# Exploring the Connection Between Children's Literature and Music

# Exploring the Connection Between Children's Literature and Music

REGINA CARLOW

**LIBRARIES**
UNLIMITED
A Member of the Greenwood Publishing Group

Westport, Connecticut • London

**Library of Congress Cataloging-in-Publication Data**

Carlow, Regina.
   Exploring the connection between children's literature and music / Regina Carlow.
      p. cm.
   Includes bibliographical references and index.
   ISBN 978-1-59158-439-1 (alk. paper)
   1. School music—Instruction and study—Activity programs.   2. Children's poetry—Study and teaching—
Activity programs.   3. Early childhood education.   I. Title.
MT10.C29     2008
372.87—dc22       2007040134

British Library Cataloguing in Publication Data is available.

Library of Congress Catalog Card Number: 2007040134
ISBN: 978-1-59158-439-1

First published in 2008

Libraries Unlimited, 88 Post Road West, Westport, CT 06881
A Member of the Greenwood Publishing Group, Inc.
www.lu.com

Printed in the United States of America

The paper used in this book complies with the
Permanent Paper Standard issued by the National
Information Standards Organization   (Z39.48–1984).

10  9  8  7  6  5  4  3  2  1

# *Contents*

Chapter 1:     Introduction                                                          1

Chapter 2:     A Rationale for Singing with Young Children                            7

Chapter 3:     Other Ways to be Musical                                             19

Chapter 4:     Working with Preschool Children                                       31

Chapter 5:     The Primary Grades: K–2                                               57

Chapter 6:     Working with the Intermediate Grades: 3–5                             83

Chapter 7:     Some Final Thoughts                                                  103

Appendix A:   Glossary of Musical Terms                                            109

Appendix B:   Tunes Used in Lesson Ideas in Chapters 4–6                           113

Appendix C:   Musical Works                                                        115

Appendix D:   Bibliography                                                         119

Index                                                                              123

# CHAPTER 1

## *Introduction*

I have been a music teacher of young children on and off for nearly twenty-five years; during which time I have conducted many children's choirs, taught general music to preschool and elementary grades, as well as worked with babies and their parents. Additionally I have taught many college students who will become teachers—childcare providers, classroom teachers and music teachers who intend to work with very young children. In my work as a choral conductor, music teacher and college professor I have often taken the medium of music as an avenue of communication for granted.

When I was a child, I sang with my family. My sisters taught me songs they had learned in school. I remember sitting on my Grandpa's knees and listening intently as he sang Neapolitan folk songs. My mother and I invented operas and added new words to familiar songs and once I started school, I began to write poetry and set the lines of rhyme to simple melodies I could play on the piano. I have always been musical and found that singing comes naturally to me—and therefore have had no difficulty in sharing my love of music and songs with my students.

I also have a love of literature. As with singing, my first memories of reading are being read to by my mother, sisters and aunts. I started reading very young and as soon as I could manage on my own, I began to take a book to bed with me, reading *Five Little Peppers and How They Grew* next to my mother. As I grew older, books provided an escape from the world—I often read three or four books simultaneously, each one engrossing me in a different capacity.

So when I became an elementary music teacher, I almost immediately began to use story books with my early childhood classes. I remember thinking gleefully: now that I'm an elementary teacher, I have an excuse to buy children's books—lots of them. And I did. My favorite books were those that lent themselves to building music lessons around them, such as *Over in the Meadow, Froggy Went a Courtin'* or *Step Back Baby*.

In the twenty-first century most early childhood specialists believe children should be taught through developmentally appropriate means, including active learning experiences, varied instructional strategies, a balance between teacher-directed and child-directed activities, an integrated curriculum and the use of learning centers. While **Developmentally Appropriate Practice** (DAP) is now a given in early childhood education, sadly, musical play is often neglected in favor of language acquisition and development in the education of young children.

Our species is hard-wired for sound; we know this because of our reflexes and visceral responses to noise. Yet as a culture, we rely on others to do music for us. It is generally believed that the development of a strong music culture is dependent upon generations of musical participation beginning in early childhood. This starts with building positive musical dispositions. These dispositions can lead to music participation in adulthood, which in turn influences how those adults will parent the next generation of children.

Unfortunately, the musical interaction and entertainment that families used to provide for one another have been replaced by the solitude of interactions with television, video games, personal music devices and other forms of electronic entertainment. This has resulted in several generations of children who have grown up quite comfortable with manipulating technology as a means to procure music, thereby surpassing a need to make music. We have become a culture of listeners—not *doers* of music. The emphasis throughout this book is to broaden the possibilities of *doing* music and in particular, singing and playing with music as a means of inviting very young children into the world of language, literature and culture.

## MUSIC: A HUMAN ACTIVITY

On their own, infants begin to explore sounds through their coos, cries and gurgles. Their experimentation in this "babble" stage is made up of exploration with vowels and consonants they may have previously heard, extending their duration, repeating them rhythmically and in rising and falling pitch passages (Campbell, 1995). Children between the ages of six to eleven months, or what is referred to as the late infancy stage, require stimulation: things to look at, touch, hear, smell and taste. Musical interaction is a natural occurrence between infant and caregiver. Higher pitched babbling or baby talk, the natural melodic contours of cries and coos, the rise and fall of speech patterns used to arouse or calm a child and repetitive patterns that are uttered by caregivers are all examples of how the nature of communication between infants and caregivers mimic musical engagements.

This interaction sets the stage for language development. This often proves to be the musical fork in the road for infants. Many suggest that an important period of musical growth is between the ages of eighteen months and three years as this is when the child is beginning to develop a repertoire of tonal patterns. Simultaneously, tonal memory is being shaped. We know that musical environment has a great effect upon a young child's musical development and that children who come from homes where the family listens to, is interested in and participates in musical activities are more naturally musical than children who don't.

Musical interactions affect a child like nothing else does. As a child performs or listens to music he or she becomes human in a unique way. Another way of thinking about humans *being in the world* with music is that music is an action; it is something that people *do*. Christopher Small points out that no matter how we take in music or do music, it adds a corporal and physical quality to our lives that combines sound with feeling and is an encounter between human beings that takes place within a physical and a cultural setting.

Patricia Shehan Campbell suggests that children find music a meaningful part of their daily lives, and they derive meaning from the music they experience. As children sing or play, they are revealing not just mere skills but also thoughts and feelings that they can convey in no other way. Music is an important means of communication that young children use intuitively; caring adults are challenged to provide exploratory and participatory music play experiences that nurture children's natural propensity for music.

Music making is one of the traits and behaviors that enhance the survival our species and is an important part of what makes us human.

Many studies suggest that music, specifically the presence of musical interaction, increases a newborn's heart rate. Consider for a moment the case of newborns in crisis, who have no access to caring interaction in their first precious months of life. The following narrative shows how baby Christina communicated that she felt safe with me. It shows how she began to "speak" as we created a song together.

### Failure to Thrive

Mike and his wife Joanna had recently become foster parents to six-month-old Christina. A week ago they were contacted by social services and had been warned that the infant had been declared failure to thrive (FTT) by a physician and needed to be placed in their home immediately. The baby had been found clearly in a medical crisis—she was underweight, dirty and had been left alone in a house with two other children under the age of four. Joanna had asked me to come and watch the child with Mike while she ran some errands several days after they had brought her home. I watched Mike hold his new charge, bouncing her gently as she let out small cries, coos and gentle gurgles. Then those sounds began to take on greater urgency. The whimpers became louder; her tiny hands began to tighten into fists. Her breathing had become irregular and her miniature arms and legs began to flail.

I watched as Mike tried to calm the infant, but he quickly became frustrated. He passed her over to me, and I held the baby in my arms. Her dark eyes showed no signs of life and her head was puffy with reddish blotches covered by a fine mass of infant hair. Her facial expression held a frightening frown, and her lips were caked with sores. Not knowing what to do, I began to imitate her sounds and I started cooing and humming back to the frightened infant using just a few notes. My voice placement was high and soft. The baby continued to wail, and I remember feeling I was humming to myself.

Then I began to improvise a few short melodies on a neutral syllable and I noted a slight shift in her body tension. I found myself searching for ways to extend the little tunes into familiar endings, and then I'd start up again, humming another familiar song. I found myself feeling a little self-conscious in front of Mike—but I persisted and in just a short while I noticed that Christina had begun to focus on me and actually responded by following the movements of my fingers with her eyes. I began to bounce her gently and tapped her tiny hands and feet as I sang.

I saw that the frown had begun to melt into a gentle line. The creases of her face had also disappeared. The baby then began to whimper again and imitate some of the same sounds I was making. Then she began to make sounds all her own; she was soon making playful coos, babbles and gurgles that displayed her participation and enjoyment of the rhythmic and melodic play between the two of us.

Why is the power of song so poignant? Why was I able to communicate through song with this clearly distressed infant? How did she know to respond to me?

## MAKING MUSIC: AN ACT OF TRUST

We know that regardless of family structure or day-to-day life experiences, children are greatly influenced by their primary caregivers and are highly motivated to please and to emulate the value system of these important people. Caregivers become the first and most important music teachers for children. Yet often, because their own perceived inability to make music, caregivers, teachers and family members who surround themselves with very young children close themselves off to the musical nature of children and instead focus on language, social and physical development, leaving the musical growth of children to specialists.

In some cases, this works. Some families do prioritize music making and some have the means to send their children to early childhood classes offered by community music schools or private studios. But by and large, this specialized training is out of reach for millions of children who make up most of the day-care and preschool populations in the United States. Often, the only music available for these children is minimal listening experiences that might involve a radio or television in the background; certainly, little if any singing occurs during the child's day. Despite what we know about the power of music as a means to build relationships, communicate feelings and provide comfort, we have sadly relegated music to an elitist realm in our schools and communities.

Perhaps this is because culture has engrained in us that there is a right way and a wrong way to be musical; this simply is not true! All adults who work with children can be musical to some degree. Making music together with children is an act of community and humanity. For children, who are born musical, it is a natural reflex and helps them make inferences about the world. However, it also requires a leap of faith for those of us who wish to lead children in being musical in their daily lives. We have to not only believe in the power of music for music's sake, we must also find ways to push beyond our fears of our own inability to "music" with children in order for them to reap the social, intellectual, physical and spiritual benefits of intentional music making in their lives.

## MUSIC BUILDS COMMUNITY

It has long been recognized that children learn best when they feel safe. It is also commonly accepted that children learn when they recognize experiences as relevant to their lives and when they are comfortable taking risks as learners. To take this one step further, children learn best when they feel as if they are part of a community in which everyone is accepted and in which individuality is encouraged. An important component of DAP involves building a caring community of engaged learners where all are valued and included.

Community can be defined as a set of interactions and expectations that have specific meaning to its members. Group music making, then, among children becomes intentional connective activity that creates specific artistic meaning to those who produce it. As children participate in musical activities together, their brains, bodies and hearts are engaged and singularly focused. As children create, perform and experience music together, they are creating a caring community.

## MUSIC ENHANCES LEARNING

John Flohr suggests there are many well-documented extrinsic benefits of the value of music in a child's life and education. These benefits include fostering motor development, promoting cultural heritage, providing release of tension, teaching language development, music as carrier of information, and using music to help teach other subjects such as reading or mathematics.

Throughout time, people have recognized and intentionally used the powerful effects of sound. The idea of using music intentionally to enhance learning has been recognized for many years by caregivers and teachers of children of all ages. In his book *Music and Learning* Chris Brewer notes that music helps:

- establish a positive learning state
- create a desired atmosphere
- build a sense of anticipation
- energize learning activities
- change brain wave states
- focus concentration
- increase attention
- improve memory
- facilitate a multi-sensory learning experience
- release tension
- enhance imagination
- align groups
- develop rapport
- provide inspiration and motivation
- add an element of fun
- accentuate theme-oriented units

Zero to Three, a nonprofit organization dedicated to advancing the healthy development of babies and young children stresses that music is a powerful means of communication in early childhood and should be utilized in almost all areas of language development. The inherent rhythmic nature of fairy tales, children's stories and chants offers many opportunities for repetition. Combining simple songs or chants with story time helps develop fluency with word patterns, word recognition and comprehension for very young children as well as beginning and more advanced readers.

Children learn to relate the information of a text through dialogue vis-à-vis the medium of music rather than pure narration. The addition of a rhythmic beat to a rhyme or chant not only helps coordination but assists in helping children learn about anticipation and speech patterns.

The following statement by the Music Educator's National Conference, an American organization that provides professional development and advocacy support for music teachers, suggests the importance of music in the child's learning process.

All children have musical potential. Every child has the potential for successful, meaningful interactions with music. The development of this potential, through numerous encounters with a wide variety of music and abundant opportunities to participate regularly in developmentally appropriate music activities, is the right of every young child.

## MAKING MUSIC TOGETHER MAKES A DIFFERENCE

Singing, playing or any other manner of making music with children can give them a sense of belonging, of shared purpose. The book is organized around the developmental needs of children, taking into consideration children's interests, physical and intellectual development and curricular concerns. After preliminary chapters discussing the musical nature of children, the ins and outs of the singing voice and exploration of various means of music making, Chapters 4 through 6 are presented by age level, stressing several approaches to the integration of children's literature and songs and musical activities.

Most of the lesson plans in these chapters were contributed by music teachers from the Albuquerque Public Schools Itinerant Elementary Music Program. While these teachers are music specialists, they have taken great care to present their lessons so they can be used in a variety of settings. Therefore, these plans are both child- and teacher-tested and can easily be adapted for use in the elementary classroom, school or public library setting or in a child care environment. Lesson plans, lesson extensions and ideas for integration across the elementary curriculum are included in each chapter.

The final chapter presents helpful suggestions for choosing a book to enhance with music. There you will find more detailed information on adapting poetry to choral reading, how to dramatize a book and more suggestions about using recorded music as a background for books. Additionally, the final chapter includes a chart that shows literary standards with musical activities.

In the appendixes I have included a glossary of musical terms, musical notation to several unfamiliar tunes should you care to learn new songs, a list of suggested musical works to look for when using recorded music and a number of suggestions for more books that go well with musical activities. Each chapter features at least one vignette that highlights children and adults playing, singing or moving to music. These vignettes are taken from my years in the classroom and are based on encounters with children and music that have helped shape my philosophy of teaching and making music. I believe that people who make music together in any form make the world a better, more human place. It is through shared musical experiences that we begin to affect change in ourselves, each other and our world.

## REFERENCES

Allen, L. Eileen, and Lynn Marotz. *By the Ages: Behavior and Development of Children Pre-birth through Eight.* Clifton Park, NY: Delmar Learning, 2000.

Andress, Barbara. *Music for Young Children.* Orlando, FL: Harcourt Brace, 1998.

Brewer, Chris. *Music and Learning: Seven Ways to Use Music in the Classroom.* Tequesta, FL: LifeSounds, 1995.

Campbell, Patricia Shehan, and Carol Scott-Kassner. *Music in Childhood: From Preschool through the Elementary Grades,* 3rd ed. New York: Schirmer, 2005.

Flohr, John W. *The Musical Lives of Young Children.* Upper Saddle River, NJ: Prentice Hall, 2005.

Jensen, Eric. A*rts with the Brain in Mind.* Alexandria, VA: Association for Supervision Curriculum and Development, 2005.

Music Educator's National Conference Position statement on early childhood education: Beliefs about young children and developmentally and individually appropriate musical experiences. 1991. www.menc.org/information/prek12/echild.html. Retrieved June 23, 2007.

Small, Christopher. *Musicking*: *The Meanings of Performing and Listening.* Middletown, CT: Wesleyan University Press, 1998.

Zero to Three. *Getting in Tune: The Magic of Music in Childcare.* 2002. www.zerotothree.org/site/DocServer/music-childcare.pdf?docID=308. Retrieved June 23, 2007.

# CHAPTER 2

# A Rationale for Singing with Young Children

Children are born **phonating** in a high and tuneful range, and their babble is inherently musical. Almost immediately, babies begin to sort out the sounds they can make with the sounds of their environment. In fact, some research suggests that children are physiologically "programmed" to sing. Shortly after birth, babies start to make sense of the sounds that they themselves produce as separate from the sounds of their surroundings. Soon after, they are able to express their delights and discomforts merely by vocalizing. A child's voice is her first toy as well as her first means to interact with other humans.

Based upon the above findings, researchers have learned that music activities are developmentally appropriate and provide most success if they take these characteristics into account. The activities for children must be based on what children can do, rather than on what adults think is fun.

## SINGING: A WAY OF MAKING SENSE WITH THE WORLD

We have many reasons to sing with children, the most important being that it is an intimacy and an acceptance of the child, a primal one. When we sing with a child, we are saying, "I honor you—your heart, your mind, your lungs, your intellect. I will share my voice with you and we will create something important."

Singing releases the insides of a child. Songs, either composed or improvised, provide children with a means to frame the world through their own ability to make meaning. Barbara Andress suggests that inside a young child are many songs, some of which are waiting to be heard by others and some of which are for the child's own special playful use. Very young children often make sense of the world by singing one or two words over and over again, repeating a loved phrase or a snappy rhyme, thoroughly enjoying the feeling of the delicious rhythm slipping over their tongues.

A child's singing may begin with a chant that he hears in his head about a small flower or a beautiful bird. He fills his lungs and speaks the chant in a high voice or a low growl. He can imitate the cries of nature around him or the sound of a car horn or a cell phone ring tone. When a child sings about what is inside of him, all parts of his body vibrate—his head, his chest. His arms raise to let the sound out, his feet move and his pulse quickens.

Songs tap into the artistic life of a child. A child who sings is expressing her inner artist as she freely allows the music to come from her, using her breath and lungs to present an artistic version of something. A child sings; therefore, she is. We know that songs that make sense to children are songs about their world. Tunes that are comfortable, the old standards ("Frere Jacques," "I'm a Little Teapot" or "Twinkle Twinkle Little Star"), help children put a frame on certain aspects of the world. We can change the words of "Teapot" or "Twinkle" and sing about chickens and lollipops. By bringing new contextual information to tunes we feel comfortable singing, we can find new and musical ways to help kids make sense of their worlds.

At least some of the standard tunes are part of our library, our My-Pod if you will. They are what we carry with us day in and day out. We can pull them up and use them throughout various scenarios in our lives. Depending on how much we sang as children, we can have as many as several hundred tunes stored in our brain. But what if we don't have a tune repertoire that is our own? Over the years, many of my college students have expressed frustration about their own abilities to sing with children. While they freely admit that all children probably have a musical orientation (including themselves as children) their own musical identities do not include being a song leader. Their own feelings and self-perceptions of their musical limitations frequently hamper their ability to sing with children.

## SINGING IS BELIEVING

What is singing? If you ask ten different people to define singing, you will get ten different answers. One man might say that singing is a confluence of breath, heart and mind; his wife might counter that it is a mental equation involving careful calculation and adjustments. For some it can be an outward man-ifestation of inner artistry; for others, it can be a physical demonstration that incites deep humiliation.

What is so frightening about singing? Singing shows our humanity in a way like no other. Singing forces us to penetrate the facade of what we want the world to see about us and shows the whole of us. Singing is a revealing and vulnerable act. It is us saying, "This is who I am. Don't you dare laugh." Some of us have been ridiculed about our voices, and some of us have never explored our voices as adults. Singing can trigger pleasant memories or it can conjure up images of shame and distrust. Be-cause of these contradictions, this physical, mental and artistic act can leave us feeling both affirmed and vulnerable. In singing, we open ourselves to the universe. In essence, this form of vulnerability strikes at the very core of who we are.

Many of us have felt insecure about our voices, or fear that our voices project an image of someone we don't want to share with the world. Some voices are pure and full-bodied, some are ragged, some suggest an imminent choking, some are earthy and dense and still others are shrill and unsure.

Yet for young children, singing is an important means of communication that they use intuitively. It is no secret that children often have no qualms about bursting into random and wonderful song cre-ations of their own. Children are spontaneous composers and improvisers of playful, joyful and simple songs. Unlike adults, they easily transcend their own perceived or unperceived limitations as singers and tend to use music as a release valve for their emotions or fantasies. Unlike adults, children find it easy to transform these fantasies into musical expressions. The following narrative highlights a moment with Beatrice, a playful six-year-old who shared her favorite song at a party.

## BE OUR GUEST

I remembered Beatrice as a shy four-year-old with blonde hair and bright blue eyes who sat in her daddy's lap through most of the sessions of her Saturday morning music class. The class had fourteen children between the ages of four and seven, and we spent our time together singing songs, playing games and instruments and dancing to music. Despite her obvious musicality, during the first few months of the class, Beatrice was often reluctant to sing and rarely participated. By the end of the year, she seemed more comfortable with risk taking and usually found the courage to join in our songs and games for at least some of the class time.

Two years later, I encountered the girl and both her parents at a party where she was the only child present. I recognized her immediately and I asked her if she still loved music. She shook her head saying, "yes," and told me she had just been in a play where she got to sing, dance and say some lines. She asked her mother if she could sing me one of the songs from the play. Her mother seemed shocked at this request from her normally shy child but expressed her positive endorsement of the after-school drama class as being a good experience for her little girl. She told her daughter that it would be fine for her to sing for us. Clearly delighted, Beatrice announced, "I have to get ready" and ran from the room.

The adults, many of us having met for the first time, made small talk. Then the little girl trotted back into the room, with shining eyes and a posture that showed anticipation and excitement. With little girl energy and fast, clipped speech, she situated her song for the adults present. While it was hard to make out her words, it was clear that the little girl believed in what she was telling us. She made elaborate hand gestures and several bows, her beautiful little face beaming and smiling as she began. Her movements were detailed and welcoming. The light in her eyes was incredible. She kept a pulse with her head and marched tiny steps. She was full of music. She began singing:

> Be our guest! Be our guest! Put our service to
> the test
> Tie your napkin 'round your neck, cherie
> And we'll provide the rest
> Soup du jour Hot hors d'oeuvres
> Why, we only live to serve
> Try the grey stuff It's delicious
> Don't believe me? Ask the dishes!

Her parents seemed somewhat embarrassed by their child's confident performance. They had never seen her so ready to take center stage. I, too, was amazed at the transformation of the shy little girl that I knew two years ago who sat in her daddy's arms on Saturday mornings to this confident musician. When she was finished, the room erupted into cheers, and her father said, "Now if we could only get her to sing in one key!" The little girl, not knowing what he meant exactly, seemed to understand that her singing was under scrutiny by the adults present. She stopped for a moment and looked at her father and ran from the room.

I believe that Beatrice was not fully cognizant of her father's words and I am equally certain that he meant no harm to his daughter. Yet it is clear that a parent's expectation or the public/cultural awareness defines what we think of as expertise and *good* and that it becomes increasingly more important as children enter school. Very young children crave affirmation, and parents and caregivers are the primary source for that. As adults dispense and withhold affirmation, they make clear to children what is good and what is not. In Beatrice's case, her father who had sat with her in her early childhood music classes, who gave her a safe place to hide when she was a preschooler, now became her judge. I am certain that scenarios like this one are the reason many of us stop singing. Suddenly we become conscious of making music and the vulnerabilities that surround it. We allow others to define us as singers or nonsingers and to pass on their fears and inadequacies about singing.

## SINGING FEARS

Despite a keen awareness that music is important to young children as a means of self-expression, and that singing is the most constant and accessible of all instruments for children, many people feel uncomfortable with singing. The act of singing (even for trained musicians) can be a revealing, frightening and an overall unpleasant experience. We assign the labels "singer" and "nonsinger" to contestants on *American Idol* and patrons at karaoke singing events. We sing along with our iPods, but really, we're just lip-syncing. In short, adults in our culture are passive listeners that do not sing. The following vignette describes a music lesson taught by two teachers of young children who had previously identified themselves as nonsingers.

### "The Music Is Here!"

It is 8:15 on a chilly morning in the Mason Childcare center on the campus of the Centennial Community College. The school sits on the edge of a small farming community in upstate New York. Two young women walk in; one is carrying a guitar in one hand and a brightly colored poster in the other. The second woman follows her through the door holding a tote bag that jingles as she walks. She carries a hula-hoop and a large soup pot under her other arm.

Fourteen preschoolers, ages four and five, are scattered around a spacious room organized in learning centers with plastic toys, stuffed animals, blocks, storybooks, sand tables and art supplies. One group of children is playing together near the sets of blocks conversing and pretending, building up and knocking down an impressive tower of blocks. Two children huddle around the art table and work with strips of fabric and pipe cleaners, which they are fastening on small paper bags to make puppets. One child is standing at the sand table with a bucket and a cup as she measures sand for the different levels for her princess castle. Another sits in a bean bag chair with headphones on listening to a Wee Sing recording; his tiny body sways back and forth. Suddenly he notices the two young women walking in the door. The little boy cries, "The music is here! The music is here!" The rest of the children turn away from their play and begin shouting, "Music time! Music time!"

The two young women are my students in a class titled "Teaching Music for Childcare Providers" at the college, and I, their teacher, am pleased the children recognize my students as "the music." The children swarm the women demanding hugs and recognition with cries of "Do I get to play the drum today?" "Can I sit with you for the story song?" "When is it my turn to sing a solo?" The two women seem flustered at first and look at me for guidance. I lead them into a quiet room and help them get ready for their thirty-minute music lesson they had prepared. When it was time for the class to begin, I watch my students take the lead in a group warm-up, encouraging the children to put their voices up in the sky like a Superman soaring through the air; then they sing, "Hello," to each child, play a rhythm game with the class, lead a short dance, teach several new songs including one with jingle bell responses and one story song. They finally end the class with a Celtic lullaby accompanied by one of the young women on her guitar.

### "I'm Not Singing!"

While the two young women described above were acting as "specialists" and music teachers, neither considered herself a trained musician, and neither felt comfortable singing alone with the children. At the start of the semester, the students in my class seemed as if they would be anything but ready to teach music to a class full of rambunctious, energetic four-year-olds. They were a diverse group of ten women with varying degrees of educational, musical and life experiences. Two of them were in their second year of college and were making preparations to transfer to a library science program at the local university; three were already working in childcare centers and taking the class for state certification. Two women were stay-at-home mothers in their late twenties who wanted to learn to be musical with their babies. One woman worked at a church, and two were freshmen just starting college for the first time, completely unsure of what degree they might pursue.

I began the first class of our semester by singing a welcome song that featured a musical hello to each student with a space in the individualized greetings for each to respond by singing their own greeting to me. Sadly, in all but one case, my tuneful *hellos* were met with nervous silence. Only one student, one of the younger women who worked part-time in a childcare center, sang "hello" back to me, but it was with a swagger and a wink to her classmates. In a class discussion shortly following the failed greeting song, all students acknowledged the importance of music in the early childhood curriculum, but one by one, each cited her discomfort in singing with children.

More dissent followed as we reviewed the syllabus when the group learned that one of the upcoming course requirements was for each student to teach an unaccompanied song from memory to the class. Only one of my students felt she had a good voice, and two flat out declared they wouldn't be singing alone in the class.

The two young women who were fresh out of high school seemed slightly more promising. Both had been members of their high school choruses but noted they felt uncomfortable singing alone. One of the older women raised her hand and asked if she could use a recording to teach her song because she, in her words had a "terrible voice." The rest of the class listened as she tearfully shared her story of being asked to mouth the words by a music teacher when she sang in her elementary school. The women preparing to be school librarians came up together at the end of the class and informed me they would be dropping the class because they were uncomfortable with the singing requirements of the course.

Yes, singing can be a connective force among humans. For children who are born musical, it is a natural reflex. For very young children, singing is as ordinary as breathing. Songs become a means to make inferences about the world. Singing with children is important because by doing so, adults reveal themselves in an intentionally artistic way. Yet there often exists a gap between the inherent musicality of children and the comfort level of singing by the adults who teach and care for them.

## SHARING OUR VOICES

If you can walk, you can dance. If you can talk, you can sing.

This oft-quoted Zimbabwean proverb suggests that singing is an extension of speaking. The premise of this book does in fact encourage this; yet there are important differences. The simplest way to describe singing is that it involves three things:

1. A source of power—**inhalation** and **exhalation**
2. **Vibration**—the act of air passing through our vocal cords
3. **Resonation**—the process by which the product of this vibration is enhanced or aggravated as it travels through the cavities of the throat and mouth.

When we hear someone singing beautifully, what is actually happening is that the source of power (the breath) is vibrating through the singer's vocal chords and the product of that vibration becomes a beautiful tone as it travels through the singer's throat and mouth. Therein lies the difficulty of singing. A very small percentage of the world is born with natural resonators, and they innately produce beautiful tones. The rest of us have to learn how to manipulate those resonators to make our singing voices pleasing.

Sometimes it is as simple as activating a yawn to let the sound out and sometimes it is more complicated. When we sing, we require more muscular control than when we speak. As we inhale our vocal cords open. When we exhale, they close. The air that pushes through the vocal chords vibrates to produce a sound. So what makes singing different from speech?

Consider the difference between a fast walker and a slow runner. While the fast walker would win a race against the slow runner, there are more muscle control demands on the slow runner. The same is true of the difference between singing and speaking. When we sing, we intentionally take more breath, exhale it purposefully in accordance to the demands of the musical phrase we want to sing and manipulate our throat and mouth to let the sound out. This process requires more muscle control, breath and thought than talking, and it takes practice! In the following sections, I offer some suggestions for ways to bridge the gap between singing and speaking. In all cases, while the exercises may be performed alone or with children, I suggest the latter because children love to experiment and play with their voices. They will be models and motivators to you as you begin to freely open up and find your voice.

## ISOLATING OUR HEAD VOICE

So how do we engage in singing when we perceive we have neither tune bank nor vocal skills? We have to find a way to experiment with sounds we already make and get in touch with the tunes in our world. Most of us are able to manipulate speaking voices in various situations—at work, at a sporting event, in a church, in a movie theater, at the dinner table, on a picnic or in a car. The key to learning to use our voices in a musical way is to become aware of the different placement of sounds we make on a daily basis.

Most adults have both a **head voice** and a **chest voice**. The chest voice is the **vocal register** typically used in everyday speech. The tonal qualities of the chest voice are usually described as being rich or full, but can also be belted or forced to make it sound powerful by shouting or screaming. Head voice refers to the higher ranges of the voice in speaking or singing; the vibrations of sung notes are felt in the head. The tonal qualities of the head voice are often described as light, airy and clear. **Falsetto** is a singing technique, usually employed by men, that produces sounds that are pitched higher than the singer's normal range, in the **treble range.**

Patricia Campbell suggests that children will tend to sing a song in the manner and style in which it is presented to them. Therefore, when singing with children who not only sing higher than adults but also hear and perceive higher sounds more clearly, it is best to sing in the head voice. Males working with young children should try for a gentle sound, producing a lighter, somewhat softer sound than the full intensity of the singer's natural singing voice. However, if you are unsure of how to sing in your head voice, you should just sing in the most comfortable register. Children do not care how you sound; high or low, they simply want to sing. It is also important to note that *all* songs can be chanted instead of sung. Chanting is indeed a musical act.

If you want to learn to use head voice I suggest the following. In order to sing in head voice, we first must isolate our upper ranges and move from our natural speaking (chest) voice to a slightly higher hemisphere. The following exercises can lead you to singing in your head voice with just a little effort and practice.

### Sounds of Nature

Once we become aware of our different vocal inflections, volumes and ways we use words, we can begin to experiment with how it feels to intentionally produce higher and lower pitches. For example, we can shiver on particular pitch when we are cold; we might imitate the wind or the sound of a coyote in the distance; we might sing with the cries of birds, the hiccups of frogs or the buzzing, rubbing sounds of locusts. No words are necessary. Simply find a way to tune into what your voice is doing. I have done this on a walk with my dog, on a trip to the zoo with a first-grade class and sitting in my back yard.

### Rhymes High and Low

After we have experimented with the various sounds, ranges and colors our voices can produce, we can concentrate on adding words. I find an easy way to practice this is to say simple rhymes with children, allowing my voice to move freely from high to low. I find they love hearing my playful exploration of my voice. They love hearing me move back and forth from my "grandma" voice to my "football coach" voice, and I am reminded what it feels like to locate the various registers of my voice. They happily join me in the adventure of manipulating and isolating the various registers of my voice. I often use the following poem as a starting place for such exploration.

> One two three four five
> Once I caught a fish alive
> Six seven eight nine ten
> Then I let him go again.
> Why did you let him go?
> Because he bit my finger so.
> Which finger did he bite?
> This little finger, on the right.

I ask the children to say the words and pat a **steady beat** on their laps to the rhyme while I manipulate my own voice up and down. Occasionally, I'll ask a child to direct me through the poem from high voice to low voice in response to his gesture.

## Letters That Sing!

A good next step is to try to make your voice follow a visual line up or down. I like to use a chalk-board and draw the letter N on the board. The height of the N is about as tall as the board itself and I ask the children to start at the bottom of the letter with me and use their voices in a **glissando** (sliding) fashion to follow my hand up to the top of the letter and down again. Then I invite children to suggest letters and as a class we "perform" their letters. We also might do the Superman soar, in which we agree on a neutral pitch, putting our arms in an outstretched "in flight" position. The children and I raise and lower our arms and follow with our voices.

## From Speech to Song in Twenty Seconds

Inhale and speak/count to twenty. Listen to yourself carefully as you are counting and try to imagine a **musical pitch** that sounds near the location of your speaking voice. Is it higher or lower? Now begin counting again. After you reach numbers eight or nine, try to switch from speaking to singing. See if you can switch to singing the rest of the numbers to one pitch. Now try to begin counting one more time, and this time sing all the numbers. If you feel like the sounds coming out of your mouth are not pleasant, try opening the back of your throat (a simple yawn will produce this) before you begin singing the numbers. Once you have sung the numbers on one pitch, try another.

## Animal Sounds

This exercise involves softly chanting a short rhyme on a comfortable pitch. I might take a simple story chant like this:

> Here is a pig fat and round.
> He uses his snout to dig up the ground.
> Here is a turkey, and a rooster, too.
> He crows with a "*Cock-a-doodle-doo!*"
> Here is a cow who gives us milk.
> Her nose is cold and soft as silk.
> Here is a sheep, "*Baa-baa*" she goes.
> She gives us the wool to make our clothes.
> Here is a peeping baby duck.
> Here is a hen that says, "*Cluck, cluck!*"

I would use a regular speaking voice for the words and use more of a singing voice for the animal sounds (italic words).

## Vocal Improvisations at Transition Times

Instead of speaking instructions, try singing them as you switch activities: "It is time to clean up" or "It is raining out side, everyone get ready for recess." "Boys and girls, come and sit in the story circle." You do not have to sing well, just sing. Sung instructions can later turn into dialogues with children that might direct questions about an activity or happening in the classroom. These improvised dialogues can begin as question-and-answer conversations initiated by the teacher and can set the stage for exploring books, poems or class activities.

## TUNING INTO CHILDREN'S VOICES

Most children's voices are higher than adult voices. One way to practice getting in the same **range** with children is to allow individual children to lead the class. I will usually start with the **Letters that**

**Sing** exercise and invite individual children to lead the exercise. I make sure to choose a child who is comfortable and confident in his/her singing voice.

### How to Teach a Song

Once we have helped our students (and ourselves) locate our singing voices, there are a number of ways to actually teach a song to children; most of them involve vocal modeling by the teacher as the primary means to transmit the song. I suggest singing the song unaccompanied as it will not only help the children focus in on the text of the song, but also help them learn the melody easily.

### Song Selection: Range

The song selection itself is a key factor in the success of the singing experience for children. First, it is important to select a song that is age appropriate. Is the range appropriate for children to sing? As infants and toddlers begin experimenting with their voices, they do not generally notice differences in pitch. When asked to sing higher or lower, they may sing louder or softer. Their voices have a very narrow range of only a few notes. Usually, a rule of thumb is that very young children have a few more notes in their range as their age. For children ages four and five, vocal range is usually five to six notes (Figure 2.1).

Few children under the age of seven are capable of singing a song covering an octave. When possible, keys should be chosen to suit the children, not the teacher or an accompanist. Through careful treatment, the vocal range of the average child will reach an octave by the age of seven or eight (see Figure 2.2). By the end of fifth grade most children should achieve a vocal range of approximately one and a half octaves (see Figure 2.3).

Often pop tunes that children hear on the radio and at home are far out of range for children's voices; they end up speaking or lip syncing along to a recording. While some teachers feel they are unable to sing unaccompanied with children (the next chapter will focus on using recordings to teach songs), it is the premise of this book that all adults can sing in some way with children. Nonetheless, if you feel that the only way you can introduce singing with your lessons is to have the students join in singing with a recording, by all means, do so! Appendix C includes a list of sing-along recordings that work well with children's voices.

### Figure 2.1. Child Vocal Range ages 4–5.

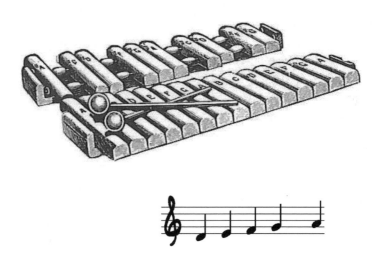

**Figure 2.2. Child Vocal Range ages 6–7.**

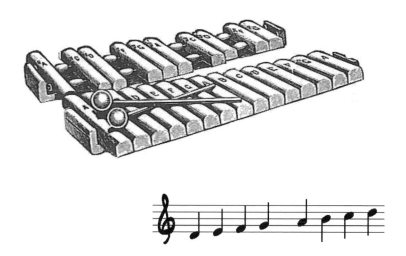

### The Sequence of Teaching a Song

When I teach a song to children, the first thing I do is create a "hook" or an interest point that the children can listen for in the song. Usually, this hook has some connection or relevance to their lives. Sometimes I'll ask leading questions. For example, I might ask "How many of you have seen a spider today?" Or I might tell the students one interesting fact about the song. "This song tells a story about a woman who had so many children all with the same name. Can you guess the name?"

Then I will sing the entire song to the class. I usually try to sing it unaccompanied, and I like to pitch the song so I'm comfortable singing it, yet it will be high enough for the children to sing along with me.

**Figure 2.3.  Child Vocal Range ages 8–11.**

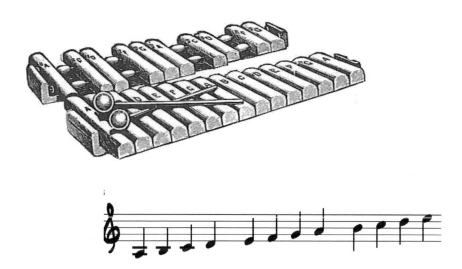

**Figure 2.4. Higher and Lower Pitches.**

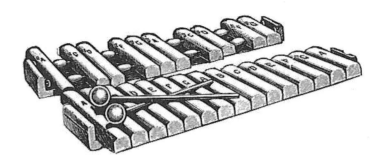

Lower Pitches                    Higher Pitches

I often check my starting note with some type of instrument. Of course a piano is best but often not available in all teaching situations. I have used a **glockenspiel** or small **xylophone** to find a starting note as well. A tip when using xylophones or other barred instruments: The smaller keys are the higher pitches. If you can match the pitches on the xylophone with your voice you might want to experiment with starting notes that fit your voice the best (see Figure 2.4).

After I sing the song through in its entirety, I will lead a short group discussion about the lyrics of the song. Usually, I will ask the children to listen for word patterns or sequences that occur in the song. Then I will sing it through again. After we have more informal discussion about the song, I will begin chunking the song, breaking it apart in smaller components. Then I will invite the children to sing the entire song with me.

### Some Ways of Echo Singing

In the case of shorter songs, I'll break the songs apart line by line and ask the children to echo me. For example:

Teacher: Here comes a bluebird through my window

Student: Here comes a bluebird through my window

Teacher: Hey diddle dum a day day day

Student: Hey diddle dum a day day day.

Children who are reluctant or unable to sing an entire phrase can often join in singing on one or two words and one tone. For example:

Teacher: Oh John the Rabbit

Student: Yes Ma'am

Sometimes we can sing an entire verse and leave out the final word tone for children to supply.

Teacher: Roll that brown jug down to town, roll that brown jug down to town, Roll that brown jug down to town so early in the . . .

Student: Morning!

Children will love to supply rhyming words to songs. For example:

Teacher: Hush little baby don't say a word, papa's going buy you a

Student: Mockingbird

Always involve the children. Ask them if anyone remembers a song that was sung the day before. Ask them if anyone remembers the words. As the children get comfortable, ask if anyone would like to show the group how the song goes. However, be careful never to put a child on the spot. Let children volunteer and contribute; you are having fun together. Singing should be something to which everyone looks forward.

## WHAT IF THEY DON'T SING?

It is usually best to invite children to sing along rather than to force them. True, there will be some children who choose not to do so at first. However, it is likely that they will eventually join if you are enthusiastic and supportive, and they see other children being successful and enjoying themselves. Try to avoid correcting the children about their singing and be careful to stay positive. If the children aren't paying attention or are being unruly, quickly close the session by happily saying that you'll sing more tomorrow.

Children will want to sing what they know. In my experience, many children have ideas for songs and will come up with suggestions to sing songs I might not know; often the songs may be too difficult to sing successfully with children. However, I try to take these suggestions seriously and I find a way to say, "Oh, that's an interesting idea. Let's try that."

The goal is for children to learn that singing is something they can really enjoy with others. When they do make an attempt (even the slightest first step), it is critical that the teacher has set them up for success rather than failure. That means the activity has to be developmentally appropriate. And it means the teacher has to appreciate, honor and accept the first attempt.

Remember, the act of singing involves the breath, the heart and the mind. Singing can release what is inside of a child. And it can help them frame the world through their own ability to spin, breathe and punctuate sounds and words. Those of us who sing with children are helping them connect with others around them. Through singing, we can help children make inferences about their world, give them a sense of belonging and a shared purpose.

# CHAPTER 3

## *Other Ways to be Musical*

We know that when working with children, it is advantageous to present information in a variety of ways, engaging all the modalities: visual, auditory and kinesthetic. Incorporating musical activities with transitions, story time and language arts lessons is a natural and musical way to help children process information. This chapter discusses a number ways to connect literacy to the multiple intelligences and abilities of children using recordings, simple rhythm instruments, rhythmic speech, sound effects and movement. These additions and treatments will enliven a lesson, convey emotive and thematic meaning and help children make important connections about what they are learning.

### Echo, Echo, Can You Hear Me?

The rambunctious class of first graders dressed for the windy, chilly weather was playing on the jungle gym right outside their classroom. Shouts and squeals of delight were heard as they pushed each other on the tire swing and made their way down the brightly colored plastic tube slides. Two little girls were making echo sounds with their voices inside a curved tunnel. "Echo, echo, can you hear me?" Their high-pitched calls to each other were interrupted by giggles and shouts from other children. One at a time two boys launched themselves down the yellow slide and played a game of tag as they ran to the overhead ladders to begin climbing.

Their teacher, Mr. Clarke, observed the rollicking recess play rituals of his first-grade class from his classroom window. Knowing that recess time was over, he signaled to the playground assistant and walked to the door leading to the playground. On his way out the door, he picked up a small hand drum, opened the door, began tapping the beat on his drum and began chanting the rhyme to "Engine Engine Number Nine." Instead of using words he used the "shh" sound.

At first, his chanting was drowned out by their shouts of excitement at seeing their teacher. But very soon they began to respond to the common beat and the first graders joined him in the chant. Some were still on swings and slides, but they chanted as a group. Mr. Clarke repeated the chant over and over with one hand on his drum, the other motioning for the children to form a line at the classroom door. They began to walk to the beat as they entered the classroom. The line leader quickly put his coat on his designated hook and took the drum from his teacher, continuing to play as his fellow first graders marched in from recess.

## CHANTING

To establish a sense of belonging in the classroom, children need to recognize themselves as members of a group that works together. Marching and chanting together in the daily ritual activities of lining up, transitioning and moving from place to place are easy entry points to musical activities that help children feel connected and centered as a community of learners. Chanting and moving with language allows children to not only hear but also interact with language in a physical way.

Just what is a chant? What distinguishes it from other types of poetry? Sonja Dunn suggests that a chant is a rhythmic group recitation. In her book on using creative chants, she recommends that we think of ourselves not so much as performers but as creative leaders, interpreting words just as we would those of a formal poem. Effective chanting in classroom and library settings gives opportunities for involvement from listeners. This is most effective with younger children who are learning to read and work with words. The pattern of the piece will lend itself to your explorations. Chanting has many of the benefits of song:

- It uses rhythm and rhyme in an enjoyable way.
- It provides patterns that can make learning easier.
- It builds children's confidence in oral language.
- It provides a change of pace and mood.
- It offers opportunities for repeated readings.
- It can serve as a writing prompt, offering students the chance to write new verses.

And in the case of Mr. Clarke's first-grade class, it provided an important community building transition time. Chants, akin to nursery and skipping rhymes, are characterized by repetition. For example, after Mr. Clarke's class has transitioned from recess to reading time vis-à-vis the "Engine Engine Number Nine" chant and march, they could readily take part in the chant "Sh, sh, sh" by Sonja Dunn from *All Together Now: 200 of Sonja Dunn's Best Chants* with its consistent repetition of the title phrase. You might want to try to create an original poem like the one below based on a story or a unit you are sharing with the children giving them an opportunity to participate verbally with easy onomatopoeic repetitions.

> Click Clack Click
> Goes the little pony
> Click Clack Click
> Go his little his little feet
> Click Clack Click
> The sound of tiny little hooves
> Click Clack Click
> Running down the street.

Chant is easily accessible for children and their participation as a group highlights the importance of clear and expressive pronunciation. Dunn notes that chanting well requires intense listening to get the right rhythm and tone and to pick up cues on time. She also suggests that chants provide a genuine opportunity for young readers to learn more about print using flip charts, sentence strips or selected words or phrases from a word wall. The very youngest children can be visually prompted through a chant with pictures.

## SETTING THE STAGE FOR RHYTHMIC SPEECH

What do we need in order to do this? All classrooms should have two things: a good set of rhythm instruments and a good sound system for playing music. Rhythm instruments that take no "expertise" other than an imagination are rhythm sticks, plastic and wood shakers, bells, gongs, hand drums, triangles and finger cymbals. Recordings that are appropriate for children should be a staple in every classroom. Recordings that highlight children's voices and light singing by adults are a must. Creating a center for **"found" instruments** as well—keys, a can of pencils, stones, rice in a jar and so on are also fun ways to activate aural and kinesthetic learning modalities. Recorded music and rhythm instruments can provide background and sound effects to a story or set a tempo for rhythmic speech.

It is important to set the stage for this creativity by setting up an environment that helps students step into the creative process gradually. Setting up "tableaux" or people sets—where on cue or signal, students strike a group pose to accentuate text. It is also helpful to allow students to suggest where and how movements should go. If students are reluctant to offer suggestions, then you might have them mirror simple movements that make sense to you.

The use of rhythmic speech is one of the easiest ways to bring a musical element into your classroom and lesson plans without singing. The simplest entry point in rhythmic speech is emotive chanting using a short rhyme, poem or song text with great inflection, drama or movements, perhaps changing your vocal inflection on important words: For example in Lewis Carroll's poem "Beautiful Soup," you might want to explore vocal inflection possibilities on the words "beautiful" and "soup":

> Beautiful Soup, so rich and green,
> Waiting in a hot tureen!
> Who for such dainties would not stoop?
> Soup of the evening, beautiful Soup!
> Soup of the evening, beautiful Soup!
> Beau-ootiful Soo-oop!
> Beau-ootiful Soo-oop!
> Soo-oop of the e—e—evening,
> Beautiful, beautiful Soup!

You might want to prepare for this activity by taking a word or phrase like circus or ice cream or rhinoceros and invite children to experiment with saying the word with different inflections and loudness or softness. Or in a more predictable rhyme, you might suggest (or elicit suggestions from the class) "staged" movements for the rhyming words while keeping a steady beat. Using Jack Prelutsky's rhymes from his collection *Ride a Purple Pelican*, I have asked children to come up with a "freeze" motion where we perform a gesture on the rhyming words and hold that motion until the next word.

You might try this with a well-known nursery rhyme like:

> Hickory Dickory *Dock*
> The mouse ran up the *clock*
> The clock struck *one*
> The mouse ran *down*
> Hickory Dickory *Dock*!

Thus, movement and pantomime on particular words and phrases are also wonderful ways to involve children on a kinesthetic level. This activity can be extended to include the use of props such as personal artifacts or meaningful objects that children bring from home or even original student artwork. Costumes, scarves, streamers and fabrics can also create a mood for text and speech play. Puppets are also a simple way to get students involved in a story—they might feel less reluctant to chant or move as a puppet character.

## REPETITION AND RHYMES

Finding repetition and patterns in the actual text are also effective for creating interest and drama in a story. You might want to take repeated patterns and add a twist or turn of your own to make it "rhyme" for children to speak or move to. For example in *Listen to the Rain* by Bill Martin Jr. and John Archambault, the phrase "listen to the rain" is repeated four times throughout the story—you might make up a chant for the class to say when those words come up in the story. For example:

> Listen to the
> Listen to the
> Listen to the rain—drippy, rain!

Finding words that "sing" or sound is an easy way to launch your students into a musical journey. Once we locate these words, we can experiment with louder and softer dynamics in our reading and interpretation. In the book *Snake Alley Band* by Elizabeth Nygaard, numerous insects, mammals and birds "speak" using musical scat.

> "Did someone say band?" Bird twirled like a top,
> Flinging feathers everywhere
> Twee-ttweedle-dee-deet, he twittered
> POP-POP-DOO-WOP, bubbled Fish
> **Cha-BOP cha-BOP cha-BOP** croaked Frog.

We can also find places in text where a word can be given greater emphasis with a "sound"—either by an instrument or a vocalization. Words like "crack," "pop" or "scrape" will suggest the insertion of sounds and can set the mood for a story. In the book *City Beats* by S. Kelly Rammell, the sounds of traffic in a city can be explored and mined for their musical opportunities:

> Honk! Beep!
> Screech! Squeak!
> Steel rails hum.
> Rattle! Swoosh!
> Zoom! Whoosh!
> Ride, fly, run!

Sometimes we can create an original chant about the story using some ideas or fragments of text. Alternatively, we can create a chant or rhyme from a particular character's words. In Ann McGovern's version of the classic story *Stone Soup* we might take the old lady's words "Soup from a stone, fancy that" and create a rhyming chant that might go like this:

> Soup from a stone fancy that—
> Soup from a stone—I'll eat my hat.
> Soup from a stone—wouldn't feed a cat.

We can then use this chant to reinforce a pattern every time the old lady speaks to the little boy in the story.

Original sound effects can be an engaging addition that can enliven a book. This could occur on words that suggest color, action, to signal theme or character. For example, in Gerald McDermott's *Musicians of the Sun,* the characters Lord of the Night, Wind and Sun can all be represented by a different sound effect—done by onomatopoeia or by using simple found or classroom instruments.

Linda Crawford suggests creating vocal and instrumental sound carpets—or soft background sounds made at the same time the reader is reading or telling the story to highlight the emotional component of a reading rather than the action. During a scary passage, the group might make ghostly sounds during the reading or at tender or sad moments, they might add quiet humming, a lullaby or other soft song. In this scenario, exploring mood, tone, pace and emotion can help create sensitive and inspired readers.

**Choral speaking** is a way to include the entire class in chanting a poem or particular section of text. Speakers or readers can be positioned around the room and can be alternated between the entire group and "solo" readers. These solos can provide an opportunity for children to experiment with contrasting vocal inflections and dynamics. Sometimes recorded background music or a drumbeat or other sound effects can add to the mood of the story.

Nancy Larrick suggests that any poem with a repeated pattern (sometimes called a refrain or "chorus") is suitable for reading aloud as a group. She uses the poem "If we walked on our hands" by Beatrice Schenk de Regniers as an example of a good alternating poem that can be effective using two separate groups. In the example below, I have used the song/poem "Yankee Doodle." This can be done placing children in two groups facing each other in conversation, one group taking the bold text lines and the other group speaking the nonbold text:

> Yankee Doodle came to town
> A-ridin' on a pony,
> He stuck a feather in his hat
> And called it macaroni!
> **Yankee Doodle keep it up,**
> **Yankee Doodle dandy.**
> **Mind the music and the steps**
> **And with the girls be handy**.
> Father and I went down to camp,
> Along with Cap'n Goodwin,
> The men and boys all stood around
> As thick as hasty puddin'
> **Yankee Doodle keep it up,**
> **Yankee Doodle dandy.**
> **Mind the music and the steps**
> **And with the girls be handy**.

## JAZZ CHANTS

**Jazz chants** are snappy, rhythmical poems and rhymes that can be said with a swinging rhythm—similar to rap or rapping. They were created by Carolyn Graham, an English as a Second Language (ESL) teacher and jazz pianist who was fascinated by the natural connection between the rhythm of spoken American English and the one-two-three-four beat of American jazz. While jazz chants were used originally for English language learners, I have found the use of these jazzy poems to be quite effective with all children, from toddlers through upper elementary grades. Students may perform these poems in small or large groups. Rhythm instruments can be added to enhance the beat, if desired.

Jazz chants are interactive. Students speak, sing, tap, stomp and move while chanting. The rhythmic presentation of the natural language is the key to success for jazz chants. The strong beat and the meaningful lines make the chant stick in one's mind. The effect doubles and triples when music, movement and role play are added.

Jazz chants are meaningful and communicative. Chanting resembles pattern drills in some ways because it is based on a combination of repetition and learner response. Although jazz chants lessons involve a great deal of repetition, the repetition is always in response to other students or the instructor and always ends with activities such as role play. With jazz chants, language learning is no longer a painful and boring repetition and memorization process but a natural and interactive process.

I have used jazz chants to enhance both a children's book and song or rhythmic learning in my music classes. There are many volumes of jazz chants by Carolyn Graham. Four of her books are cited at the end of this chapter.

"Where's Jack?" from Graham's *Jazz Chants for Children* is a versatile chant that introduces rhyming words—know and go, there and chair—presents the structures of "wh" questions, positive and negative responses and two verb tenses (present and past tenses). The chant also teaches the function of asking for whereabouts and responding to questions. It is perfect for pair work and role play.

> Where's Jack?
> He's not here.

Where did he go?
I don't know.
Where's Mary?
She's not here.
Where did she go?
I don't know . . .

### Steps in Teaching a Jazz Chant

1. Be sure students know all the key vocabulary.
2. Write the chant on the board.
3. Read the entire chant to the class.
4. Read one line at a time and have students repeat the line until they can say most of the words.
5. Add the rhythm (clapping, marching, pounding the table or a drum). Let the class do the rhythm and say it at the same time.
6. Let "soloists" say it while everyone else claps.

## USING RHYTHM INSTRUMENTS

Every classroom or community space for children should have a box of unpitched rhythm instruments. But even prior to using traditional rhythm instruments, children and adults can begin to explore sounds they can make with their bodies. Children all over the world have been experimenting with clapping, snapping, tapping, stomping, patting and sound that they can make from their bodies. This is called **body percussion** and is an easy musical connection to make with reading.

### Body Percussion

One way to work with body percussion is to take a speech pattern perhaps from a familiar rhyme and transfer the rhythm of the words to one level of body percussion. For example, try clapping the rhythm of the words of "Hickory Dickory Dock." Now clap the phrase again and stomp on the word "dock."

This skill can be transferred to a book or poem with repetitive phrases. For example, in "Listen to the Rain" the words can be performed on body percussion with hands rubbing together to the rhythm of the word at each entrance of "Listen to the Rain." Body percussion can also function as a point of departure for individual or small group composition using a book like Brian Pinkney's *Max Found Two Sticks*.

Pat pat pat . . .
Putter putter pat tat
Tap tap tap
Dum Dum . . . dum-de-dum
Thump di-di Thump. Thump di-di Thump.

The text can be used to experiment with various sounds children could make through body percussion using claps, stomps, pats and slaps. A logical next step would be to take the same text and use "found" instruments. For example, a large plastic garbage can makes a great bass drum. Water cooler jugs, buckets and cardboard boxes make higher-pitched drum sounds as well. Various shakers can be created with assorted bottles full of rice, beans or gravel. Old keys, suspended one by one from a stick, can become a set of chimes.

Keys in a tin can or metal box can produce an entirely different effect. Pan lids of various sizes and shapes produce beautiful sounds when struck on the edge of the lid. Cans, metal chairs and desks can be used to create contrasting sounds as well. Linda Crawford suggests creating what she calls stone rhythms in which all students have two stones in which they first experiment with the sounds they can make which later grow into individual rhythm patterns.

As you preview the story, look for places where sound enhancements such as body percussion or instruments might add to the meaning of the words or picture. Sometimes illustrations might suggest sounds even when words do not mention those elements. In *Papagayo the Mischief Maker* by Gerald McDermott, the vivid illustrations of animals in the rainforest might suggest sound effects created by traditional, found or body percussion instrument.

## Sound Carpets

Sometimes story time can be enhanced by adding **sound carpets,** a soft background sound made while reading a story. These sounds can create a mood or convey emotion about a particular story. The use of sound carpets as background sounds can be an effective way to communicate author's intent as well as a means to involve students in the process of making meaning of the story. Certain instruments or sounds can be used to signal a character's entrance, speaking or exit. A rainforest environmental sound carpet might include the following sounds:

- A rainstick—or a tall jar of rice or sand in a bottle
- A slide whistle or kazoo using soft, high pitches
- Soft hand drumming—using brush strokes instead of taps
- Castanets or small finger cymbals
- Vocal sounds imitating wind or animal noises

## A Sample Sound Carpet

Traditional instruments such as bells, small shakers, triangles or finger cymbals can be used to create a sound carpet for the Mother Goose rhyme "A Farmer Went Riding"

> A farmer went riding
> Upon his gray mare
> Bumpety, bumpety, bump!
> With his daughter behind him,
> So rosy and fair,
> Lumpety, lumpety, lump!
>
> A raven cried "Croak!"
> And they all tumbled down,
> Bumpety, bumpety, bump!
> The mare broke her knees
> And the farmer his crown,
> Lumpety, lumpety, lump!
>
> The mischevious raven
> Flew laughing away,
> Bumpety, bumpety, bump!
> And vowed he would serve them
> The same the next day,
> Lumpety, lumpety, lump!

Recordings of natural sounds can add a sensory dimension to studying the rainforest. There is a wide selection of environmental-type recordings on the market today that you may wish to purchase, but the following activity is a way that you and your students can create your own indoor thunderstorm.

### Creating a Thunderstorm

1. Have students sit cross-legged in a circle or semi-circle.
2. Start by quietly rubbing your palms together, making a soft rustling sound.
3. Add students one by one—either by seat order or by teacher eye contact.
4. When everyone is rubbing his or her palms, begin snapping your fingers.
5. Follow finger snapping by patting your hands on your legs and finally by stamping your feet.
6. As the storm subsides go through the first three steps in reverse order, patting legs, snapping fingers, rubbing palms.

## INTEGRATING MOVEMENT

It is a given that children love to move and most do so naturally from birth with or without music. Infants begin rocking and waving, and as children mature physically, they begin to jump, hop, stamp, sway and snap to beats in their own musical worlds. Movement, then, is a logical and joyful addition to a lesson, story time session or activity. From the perspective of child development, movement is the essence of children's play and the manner through which many of them come to know their world. When considering a movement activity with children make sure you have:

- Physical space to move—push chairs and desks to the side, select an open space or move outside.
- If you can't move the furniture or move the activity outside, consider the options of moving in tight spaces—what can you do sitting down? What can you do with only a few steps to the right or to the left?
- Be sure to set movement rules. I like to install a "safety check" so that children can regulate their movements within certain boundaries that make sense to them.

I like using the piano for playing background music but have also had much success using recordings. I keep a variety of recorded music of various styles, moods and cultures on hand so that children will have many options for movement to music.

Phyllis Weikart, a noted authority on physical education and recreational dance in early childhood, suggests that there are key experiences that benefit children in school and life—thus helping them make connections with the world through a kinesthetic experience. They are:

- Following movement directions
- Describing movements using language
- Moving the body in **nonlocomotor** ways (movements that the body can perform without moving around)
- Moving the body in **locomotor** ways (walking and jumping, etc.)
- Moving with objects
- Expressing creativity in movement
- Feeling and expressing beat
- Moving with others to a common beat

In order to help children develop motor skills in early childhood, linguistic cues and verbal directions that are attached to or borne from movements are an essential part of the development of gross motor skills. Children learn to respond by aural, visual and tactile decoding. The song "Head, Shoulders, Knees and Toes" is a good example of an activity that supports these key experiences. The text of the song is sung or chanted by the teacher who is also modeling the action required for the children.

> Head, shoulders, knees and toes, knees and toes.
> Head, shoulders, knees and toes, knees and toes.
> My eyes, my ears, my mouth, my nose
> Head, shoulders, knees and toes, knees and toes!

When children are encouraged to verbalize or talk about the movements as they do them, they are developing a deeper kinesthetic awareness. By helping children develop language and vocabulary for movements, we are helping them connect language and motor performance. Weikart suggests that this is done in four steps:

1. **To talk about or describe what one is doing in movement bringing a motor act to a conscious level.** This occurs when the children sing and tap various body parts in "Head, Shoulders, Knees and Toes."
2. **To plan what one is going to do.** This step might involve a response to a piece of literature or poem—inviting the children to show a motion or make a movement when a character appears in a story.
3. **To recall the movement that has just occurred.** Children could use language to describe the movement of a character.
4. To **link a single movement to a single word.** This can be done using simple locomotor commands such as:

> Walk walk walk walk
> Running running running walk.

The teacher might combine these commands to refer to a specific character in a book—assigning specific children to walk, run and so on when the characters appear in story. There are many ways to incorporate nonlocomotor movements throughout the curriculum. Instructing children to draw letters of the alphabet in the air with their arms or to curl into a particular shape are simple ways to begin exploring nonlocomotor movements. Another option for moving in place is to seat each child in a chair and invite them to move freely in chairs to recorded music. Your instructions might be "When you hear the music start, move all of your body. When the music stops you stop."

Locomotor movements such as "walk, leap, lunge, hop, skip, run" can be easily incorporated into a lesson built around a story. For example in Eric Carle's *The Very Busy Spider* these movements are suggested by the main characters in the book.

> "Maa! Maa!" said the goat.
> "Want to jump on the rocks?"
> "Oink! Oink!" grunted the pig.
> "Want to roll in the mud?"

You might want to combine both locomotor and nonlocomotor movements using the same book with the continual refrain suggesting in-place motions or gestures.

> "The spider didn't answer. She was very busy spinning her web."

Once you are certain the children understand the task you might invite individual children to demonstrate movements for everyone to copy. Have children work in pairs so that one child takes the responsibility for selecting the movement or the position of the arms or legs and the other child follows. Then have them change roles. Use subgroups of three or four children in which a child can carry out this leadership function. Then ask an individual child to lead the entire group.

Moving with scarves is an example of moving with objects. In the rhyme "Good Morning Merry Sunshine," scarves can be used to show movement, show action or interpret the mood of the poem.

> Good morning merry sunshine.
> How did you wake so soon?
> You've scared the little stars away
> And shined away the moon;
> I saw you go to sleep last night,
> Before I ceased my playing,
> How did you get way over here
> And where have you been staying?

Paper plates under each foot can be used as imaginary skates, allowing children to portray themselves as the characters the Little Grey Rabbit, Hare or Squirrel in the book *Squirrel Goes Skating* by Allison Uttley. Children can be invited to move "like" a character in a book. Again, using Carle's *The Very Busy Spider,* children can use the animal characters of the horse, the cow, the sheep and the goat as starting points for creative movements.

There are many ways to incorporate feeling and expressing beat with children's literature. The beat is a steady ongoing pulse that occurs when a chant or nursery rhyme is recited, a song is sung or a musical selection is played. Marching or walking to a sung or spoken chant is an easy way to help children make connections to the text.

## MOVEMENT ACTIVITIES WITH OLDER CHILDREN

As children move past early childhood and into the intermediate grades, their small muscle coordination increases, and they are able to more accurately reproduce rhythms by chanting, tapping, patting, clapping and stepping. With practice, older children can do these movement activities simultaneously.

### Buffalo Soldiers

Mrs. Anderson's fourth grade class was already in place for their sharing when I entered the room. The twenty-eight children were arranged in rows of four across and seven deep. They were sitting cross-legged on the floor while their teacher reviewed the poem and step with them. Then with a wave of her hand they stood up and shook hands with their classmate directly to the side and behind as they got ready to present the chant they had created with their teacher. I was surprised to see that simply by a cue from their teacher the children had started stepping in time with each other. Then they began to clap a simple pattern in unison.

> Clap Clap Tap.
> Tap—Step forward.
> Touch and back and turn.

The class moved forward row by row—each group of four having its own stanza of the chant they had created. After they had finished their chant and step dance, they gathered around their teacher as she read *The Zebra Riding Cowboy*, by Angela Shelf Medearis, a story about cowboys in the American Southwest.

Their teacher, Gloria Anderson, did not consider herself a musician but participated in the praise dance team at her church. The creation and presentation of the step chant was a way that she could share a significant part of her own culture and musical identity with her students. Her love of dance and African American history led her to find a way to integrate her social studies and language arts curriculum with her students in a sphere that she felt comfortable—movement and dance. By sharing something important about herself to her class, Gloria was able to go deeper in her teaching and to evoke what Parker Palmer calls a capacity of connectedness that occurs when teachers join self, subject and students in the fabric of life.

Regardless of the curriculum, children should be given the opportunity to express themselves through movement, whether it is creative or structured. Creating musical environments so that children have the freedom to test their ideas will also contribute to a greater awareness and understanding of music. Parameters set within these musical environments can give children opportunities to use their imaginations as they move and sing in improvised activities. Children can be guided in structured activities as they experience movement elements such as locomotor/nonlocomotor movements and shared/personal space.

## REFERENCES

Campbell, Patricia Shehan, and Carol Scott-Kassner. *Music in Childhood: From Preschool through the Elementary Grades,* 3rd ed. Belmont, CA: Thomson Learning, 2005.

Carle, Eric. *The Very Busy Spider.* New York: Philomel Books, 1984.

Carroll, Lewis. *Alice's Adventures in Wonderland.* New York: Sterling, 2005.

Crawford, Linda. *Lively Learning: Using the Arts to Teach the K–8 Curriculum.* Greenfield, MA: Northeast Foundation for Children, 2004.

Dunn, Sonja. *All Together Now: 200 of Sonja Dunn's Best Chants.* Markham, Ontario: Pembroke, 1999.

Graham, Carolyn. *Jazz Chants*: *Fairy Tales.* New York: Oxford University Press, 1988.

Graham, Carolyn. *Jazz Chants: Old and New.* New York: Oxford University Press, 2001.

Graham, Carolyn. *Jazz Chants: Rhythms of American English for Students of English as a Second Language.* New York: Oxford University Press, 1979.

Graham, Carolyn. *Small Talk: More Jazz Chants.* New York: Oxford University Press, 1986.

Hines, Anna Grossnickle. "Do You Know Green," from *A Year in Poems and Quilts.* New York: Harper Trophy, 2003.

Katz, Bobbi. *A Rumpus of Rhymes.* New York: Dutton's Children's Books, 2001.

Larrick, Nancy. *Let's Do a Poem! Introducing Poetry to Children through Listening, Singing, Chanting, Impromptu Choral Reading, Body Movement, Dance and Dramatization.* Lakewood, WA: Great Buy Books, 1991.

Martin, Bill, Jr., and John Archambault. *Listen to the Rain.* New York: Henry Holt, 1988.

McDermott, Gerald. *Musicians of the Sun.* New York: Simon and Schuster, 1997.

McDermott, Gerald. *Papagayo the Mischief Maker.* New York: Windmill Books, 1980.

McGovern, Ann, Winslow Pinn, and Ey Pels. *Stone Soup.* Danbury, CT: Scholastic Paperbacks, 1986.

Nygaard, Elizabeth, and Betsey Lewin. *Snake Alley Band.* New York: Doubleday Books for Young Readers, 1998.

Palmer, Parker. *The Courage to Teach.* New York: Harper Collins, 1993.

Pinkney, Brian. *Max Found Two Sticks.* New York: Simon and Schuster, 1994.

Prelutsky, Jack. *Ride a Purple Pelican.* New York: Harper Collins, 1986.

Rammell, S. Kelly, and Jeanette Canyon. *City Beats: A Hip-hoppy Pigeon Poem.* Nevada City, CA: Dawn Publications, 2006.

Uttley, Allison, and Margaret Tempest. *Squirrel Goes Skating.* New York: Harper Collins, 1993.

Weikart, Phyllis. *Round the Circle: Key Experiences in Movement for Children*, Ypsilanti, MI: High/Scope Press, 1987.

Wright, Blanche Fisher. *The Original Mother Goose.* Philadelphia: Running Press Books, 1992.

# CHAPTER 4

## *Working with Preschool Children*

In our work with the very youngest children, we must keep in mind that they need many ways to explore the world. Simply put, music is an important means to do so. We also need to remember that children possess a wealth of original, unstructured versions of songs in their heads and hearts. They do not question the musical validity of what they sing because early childhood is truly a time of heartfelt musical expression and children are not bound by perceptions of their limitations.

We know that sound educational practice promotes starting at the child's level and then guiding his or her progress along the learning continuum. To enter a child's musical world means that we as teachers, librarians, caregivers and parents must find ways to value and participate in song-play, musical dialogues and improvised tone conversations that are a natural part of the culture of childhood.

### Sleep Baby Sleep

Three-year-old Damien sits on the carpeted floor of the library. Colorful plastic rattles, shakers and jingle bells surround him. His curly brown ringlets frame his chubby round face as he studies a small pink and purple shaker in the shape of an elephant. Other children are scattered on the floor nearby quietly playing with blocks, rattles and small stuffed animals. A recording of the Spanish lullaby "A la Nanita" is playing softly in the background. The singer on the recording is a woman with a light voice and she is accompanied by a guitar.

When the song ends, Miss Sally, the children's librarian begins a song conversation with the group of toddlers. Her voice is light and soft as she sings on one note, "I have a new friend who wants to meet you." (She takes a small teddy bear from behind her back.) "His name is Marco. Marco is tired and wants us to sing him to sleep." (The teacher now cradles Marco in her arms.) "What shall we sing to Marco?" Without hesitation, Damien answers "We sing sleep baby." Miss Sally says, "Let us sing Damien's song to Marco the bear." She improvises a song using the words "sleep baby sleep" and rocks Marco the bear in her arms. Damien begins to rock his plastic shaker in his arms slowly, singing the words "sleep baby sleep." Next, Miss Sally says, "I know a poem that you might like."

> Sleep, baby, sleep
> Your father tends the sheep
> Your mother shakes the dreamland tree
> And from it fall sweet dreams for thee
> Sleep, baby, sleep
> Sleep, baby, sleep

> Sleep, baby, sleep
> Our cottage vale is deep
> The little lamb is on the green
> With snowy fleece so soft and clean
> Sleep, baby, sleep
> Sleep, baby, sleep.

Miss Sally recites the poem and sings "Sleep Baby Sleep," a traditional nursery rhyme using Damien's created song pattern. Soon, Damien is singing along with his teacher, fully engaged in his song.

Song conversations like the one above are an excellent opportunity to begin musical improvisation with children. In addition to acting as a pathway to singing and chanting, these conversations can invite children to be musically inventive as they experiment with fragments of melody and bits of vocabulary. At first, these song conversations may take the form of one-sided monologues sung by teachers or caregivers while children take in the information being sung to them. Eventually, as they begin making internal connections to what is being sung, children often move into free singing, sometimes inventing wonderful songs and poems on their own.

Yet many children who spend their early months in childcare do not have the luxury of consistent one-on-one interaction with a significant adult. Sadly, musical development in early childhood settings in many instances is often overlooked—especially in the daily lives of children under the age of three. Often, it is because the adults who care for them feel inadequate musically.

Vocal development is not necessarily bound by time, but experience with and exposure to singing is an important ingredient in the first few years of a child's life. While research clearly shows that an important period of musical growth is between the ages of eighteen months and three years of age generally, the main emphasis in most early childhood programs is on the acquisition and expansion of spoken language. Yet children at this age are often the most creative, spontaneous and persistent music makers—more so than at any other time in their lives. Music making for a preschool aged child is not unusual, unique or extraordinary—it is simply what they do.

As children develop as communicators, their verbal, physical and musical skills grow too. Barbara Andress suggests important learning takes place via a three-phase cycle including:

1. hands-on experiences,
2. meaningful visual and pictorial representations,
3. and finally, mutually agreed-upon symbolic representations of ideas.

Which content to select and how to proceed depends on each individual child's developmental level. While it is obvious that all children in a given age group are not at the same developmental stage because of an infinite number of individual differences, in the paragraphs below, I describe typical musical responses and behaviors for children from ages two to four.

## SINGING WITH TODDLERS

Children around the age of two are beginning to recognize the difference between musical and non-musical sounds. Once they are able to do this, they can begin to make up their own sounds—using nonsense syllables. They are also able to sing one or two word songs. They might sing a song about a "kitty cat" or "doggie dog" or a "fishy fish" that represents a main character or idea in a story. In the book, *Jump Frog Jump*, by Robert Kalan, the phrase "Jump, Frog, Jump" can be used as a chant or simple song. For example, the teacher reads:

> This is the fly that climbed out of the water
> This is the frog that was under the fly

that climbed out of the water.
How did the frog catch the fly?
Children respond—singing or chanting: "Jump, frog, jump!"

**Fingerplays** are important for toddlers as well. First, such play involving movement of fingers, hands and other parts of the body develops kinesthetic awareness and muscular coordination. There are other benefits as well. For example, the fingerplay song "Where Is Thumbkin?" is a perfect vehicle to help children connect the context of what they know (their fingers) to more vocabulary and the social interaction of a spoken greeting. Additionally, since most fingerplays are led by adult caregivers or teachers, the opportunity of imitation, eye contact and shared expressions of silliness all stimulate activity and encourage character development.

As children turn three they become more able to vocally reproduce a recognizable song. A three-year-old can sing the following song almost all the way through.

> I'm a little teapot short and stout,
> Here is my handle and here is my spout
> When I get all steamed up then I shout,
> Just tip me over and pour me out!

It is easiest for children to sing when they can start on their own comfortable pitch. Usually this is higher than many adults sing. If you feel uncomfortable singing, try chanting the words to the rhyme softly and experimenting with higher and lower vocal inflections.

Because three-year-olds are natural mimics, they may easily reproduce the lyrics from an entire song from a recording, movie or television show with a very high level of rhythmic accuracy. At age three, children are starting to match pitches when singing with others and they are readily able to create dynamics with their voices. Three-year-olds love to participate in hands-on play with small props or to imitate adults who are singing and chanting with them.

Two- and three-year-olds are able to create their own spontaneous songs as an outgrowth of motor activities and language play. Often these songs are based on what some call the **teasing chant** such as in "Rain Rain Go Away." Likewise, many toddlers regard group singing experiences as an opportunity to listen without joining in. Some times when they do sing, they tend to lag behind a bit—or will only chime in on certain words. For example: in the song "She'll Be Coming Round the Mountain" a shy two-year-old might sing "When she comes" or "Round the mountain" over and over—either during the song or at other times.

Two- and three-year-olds are able to differentiate between speaking and singing. They can sing lullabies softly and switch to singing loudly when the lyrics of the song suggest a different action. As in the story about Damien, children can create simple lullabies with one or two words—and sing them comfortably. They can also modulate the dynamics of their speaking voices as well. With the children's book *Lullabyhullaballoo* by Mick Inkpen, a three-year-old will enjoy demonstrating the intentional use of differing vocal dynamic levels.

> A dragon is roaring.
> What shall we do?
> He's hissing and snorting!
> What shall we do?
> Tell him to SSSH!
> That's what we'll do.
> SSSH!
> Who Me?
> YES YOU!!!!!

Four-year-olds are still quite happy to make up their own songs but bring more imagination and logic to a song. They are beginning to demonstrate awareness of the differences between singing something quickly or slowly and are aware of loud and soft as well as differences in the structure or form of a song. Barbara Andress suggests that four-year-olds are sometimes able to create an improvised song when seeing a visualization of a story.

## PLAYING INSTRUMENTS

Body touch songs and chants are an excellent way to prepare children for using instruments. This chant "My Thumbs Are Starting to Wiggle" (sometimes sung to the tune of "The Bear Went over the Mountain") helps children associate what they know about their hands, feet, fingers and thumbs with exaggerated wiggles and shakes.

> My thumbs are starting to wiggle
> My thumbs are starting to wiggle
> My thumbs are starting to wiggle
> Around and around and around!
> My hands are starting to wiggle . . .
> My legs are starting to wiggle . . .
> My feet are starting to wiggle . . .

Toddlers are fascinated with the sounds that are made by traditional and nontraditional instruments. They love to strum guitars, pat drums, shake maracas and press down random keys on the piano or electronic keyboards. They especially love to "accompany" an adult who is playing one of these instruments.

They can use movement to describe obvious ideas in sung or recorded music, can stomp for loud or tiptoe for soft music. Two-year-olds tend to respond actively and enthusiastically to rhythmic listening examples such as a lively march or a dance—each at his or her own tempo. I've used the "Bounce" game with tiny stuffed animals, inviting the children to bounce their special friend on their laps along with me or a piece of recorded music.

Toddlers enjoy inventing movements that can be copied by others. While sometimes they can be shy, I find a little encouragement and enthusiasm will help a child feel comfortable leading a motion for the whole group. Two- and three-year-olds will adopt a much faster tempo or movement than might feel comfortable for adults. And they will generally not be able to synchronize their movements with a steady beat, instead moving, waving, jumping or clapping freely. This form of movement is a natural development in spatial awareness and should be should be encouraged.

Toddlers have to learn to intentionally "stop and go" using movements. The "Stop and Go" game I like to use is a chant:

> We're gonna go go go
> We're gonna go go go
> We're gonna go go go AND Stop!

Sometimes I'll accompany myself on a small drum, other times, I might use finger cymbals or claves on the word "stop." Then I'll substitute for the word "go" with "walk" or "run":

> We're gonna run, run, run,
> We're gonna run, run, run,
> We're gonna run, run, run AND Stop!

The possibilities are endless; toddlers will love playing this game and it can be used to set up a story, direction following or even as a prerequisite for playing instruments.

When using instruments with very young children, be aware that they will need time to explore the many different sounds and possibilities that can be produced. Providing unstructured time for free play and exploration with instruments will help children explore tone color, long and short sounds, high and low sounds, patterns of sound and loud and soft sounds. I like to start all my lessons with toddlers featuring a free play or exploration time with a group of child-friendly instruments in the center of a circle where children may freely and imaginatively investigate them. Rhythm instruments for young children may be purchased in sets and are usually reasonably priced, sturdy and made in brightly colored plastic and light woods so they are child-friendly. A rhythm instrument set for preschool may include:

| Triangles | Claves | Ankle bells |
| Wrist bells | Rhythm sticks | Finger cymbals |
| Xylophones | Sand blocks | Shakers |
| Mini rainsticks | Plastic handbells | Mini gongs |

By age three, children will have more coordination with mallets, drum beaters and other instruments that require striking up and down. A good preparation for this is to have children do many patting and tapping games one-on-one. Allow children to lag behind and to set their own pace with these games.

## USING RECORDED MUSIC WITH TODDLERS

There is a wealth of wonderful recorded music to use with children available—but often (like children's books) specific recordings have a very short shelf life and are difficult to locate. Yet the advent of personal music systems and the ease of legal music downloading from the Internet have made virtually all musical recordings available to us at the click of a button. Granted, many of us haven't made the switch from audio tapes and CDs, to MP3 players and iPods; and for those of us who still remember LPs and 45s, there are many wonderful recording resources to explore. In Appendix C you will find a list of classical titles that are excellent for creating mood, encouraging movement and extra suspense in a story.

With very young children it is best to avoid very loud music. But it is important to choose a wide variety of styles and tempi that includes both instruments and voices. Repeated listening will help children become familiar with patterns in the music. Because young children have trouble focusing and centering on more than one musical idea at time, it is best to present simple, easily identifiable characteristics. You might select smaller instrumental groupings or a piece with an easily discernible solo—such as a drum or banjo playing. Unaccompanied singing or singing with one or two accompanying instruments will help children connect with lyrics or the mood of a piece of vocal music.

When playing a recorded selection for toddlers, teacher eye contact coupled with modeling hand or simple body movements will help children stay focused. My rule for listening to a piece of music is "no talking during the music," and I work hard to model it for children. Again, eye contact and something to do during the music helps center the children on the listening.

An engaging prop to help children listen to recorded music is a hand puppet, toy or visual that depicts a story or directs the listening. You might want to take a familiar tune such as "The Dance of the Sugar Plum Fairy" from the *Nutcracker Suite* by Tchaikovsky and use dancing puppets to guide the listening experience. The duration is also important—I often start with a thirty-second listening example with toddlers and repeat it several times throughout the lesson. Live performances are an excellent means to help children focus on the listening experience as well. I've arranged "instrument petting zoos" with local musicians who allow the children to come up before and after a short performance and explore an instrument.

## LULLABIES: THE PERFECT ENDING

Lullabies provide a joyful, soul-soothing way to calm a child or to help lull her to sleep (and to calm ourselves at the same time), providing quiet moments of connection. Cross-culturally, lullabies are associated with parents or caregivers calming children, putting them to sleep or simply spending time together. The simple lyrics, nature and storyline of lullabies are usually intended for children and are therefore suitable for them.

I have sung many lullabies to children—some of my favorites include those I remember from my childhood. Week after week, children have asked me to sing "The Little Horsies" or "Hush." Because preschool-aged children thrive in an environment that includes repetition, routines and rituals, I like to pattern my lesson plans predictably ending each session with a lullaby song or story. Each child is given a small stuffed animal to rock or hold during the final activity. I find that these final moments in the lesson provide great opportunities for toddlers to both participate as a child and as a caregiver through songs and stories. The following stories are excellent "enders" for lessons with toddlers and can be an engaging springboard to a lullaby song or poem.

In the book *Goodnight Moon* by Margaret Wise Brown, you can invite the children to notice and respond to the color and the black-and-white illustrations (by Clement Hurd). I would tell them to listen to the reader during the color pages and quietly explore selected instruments during the black-and-white illustrated pages. For this exploration, I would use instruments with softer and tinkling tone colors, such as jingle bells, triangles, finger cymbals and small shakers.

The traditional folk song about gifts a mother promises her child is used as a departure point for the book *Hush Little Baby* by Sylvia Long. The text includes the following vocabulary paired with illustrations: hummingbird, cricket, shooting star, lightning bug, banjo and harvest moon. In my preview of the book, I share the illustrations and ask children to come up with sounds that represent the drawings and text. Similarly, I invite children to come up with sounds that represent the different animals and their babies in Mem Fox's *Time for Bed*.

## LESSON IDEAS FOR PRESCHOOL CHILDREN

In the following pages, I will present sample lesson ideas for toddlers and preschool-aged children. These lessons are inspired by lesson plans by two extraordinary early childhood music specialists, Julia Church Hoffman and Carla Haynes. All of the plans would work well in a preschool class, for a traditional library story time structure, in a childcare setting or one on one between a parent and child. In most cases, the songs are based on traditional familiar tunes—such as "The Farmer in the Dell," "Are You Sleeping?" and "If You're Happy and You Know It." In a few instances, I have included less familiar tunes for which you will find musical notation in Appendix B.

Each lesson is built on at least one children's book and contains simple musical activities, poems and movement games that teachers or caregivers can easily incorporate into their lesson plans and story time sessions. Each lesson is set up to meet both early literacy goals based on the American Library Association's Information Literacy Objectives and musical goals based on the National Standards for Music Education.

## GROUP A: BEARS EVERYWHERE!

### Lesson 1 by Julia Church Hoffman

#### *Book/Literature Selection*

*Berlioz the Bear,* by Jan Brett

*Early Literacy Goals*

Predictions and patterns

Reinforcing concepts of print

*Musical Goals*

Listening to and improvising movement to recorded music

Exploration of instruments

*Materials/Resources Needed*

A recording of *Flight of the Bumblebee* by Rimsky-Korsakov

Assorted rhythm instruments

*Berlioz the Bear,* by Jan Brett

1. FOCUS. While teacher chants the following poem, teacher models and invites children to perform suggested motions and steps.

> Teddy Bear, Teddy Bear, turn around
> Teddy Bear, Teddy Bear, touch the ground
> Teddy Bear, Teddy Bear, shine your shoe
> Teddy Bear, Teddy Bear, that will do.
> Teddy Bear, Teddy Bear, walk upstairs;
> Teddy Bear, Teddy Bear, say your prayers.
> Teddy Bear, Teddy Bear, switch off your light;
> Teddy Bear, Teddy Bear, say good night!

Children and teacher now sit in story time circle.

2. BODY OF LESSON. Teacher shows illustrations from the story and invites children to make predictions about what will come next.

3. Teacher draws attention to the music on Berlioz's music stand at the end of the book. Play *The Flight of the Bumblebee.* Invite children to move like bees during the recording—first with "bee hands," then with their bodies (the listening selection is quite short and the chaos won't last long!). Read the story—add instruments for each new character.

4. Read the story—adding instruments that students select to represent each new character. Note: Some two- and three-year-olds will be ready to hear the entire story—and some will not.

5. CLOSURE. Rock or gently bounce teddy bears (or other small stuffed animals friends) as teacher sings a short lullaby.

## 6. LESSON EXTENSIONS

A. Teach children the poem "Big Bear" using italic words—teacher and children come up with motions that are suggested by text.

> Big bear, big bear
> Hunting near the trees.
> Feasting on the honeycomb
> Made by busy bees. (*bzzz, bzzz, bzzz*)
> Big bear, big bear,
> Wading in the lake.
> Fish is your favorite dish;
> Which one will you take? (*swish, swish, swish*)
> Big bear, big bear
> Resting in your den.
> Sleeping through the winter
> Before you're out again. (*zzz, zzz, zzz*)

### Lesson 2 by Julia Church Hoffman

#### *Book/Literature Selection*

*We're Going on a Bear Hunt,* by Michael Rosen and Helen Oxenbury

#### *Early Literacy Goals*

Print awareness

Phonological awareness

#### *Musical Goals*

Perform steady beat

Improvise movement

Vocal exploration

#### *Materials/Resources Needed*

Drum

Various percussion instruments

1. FOCUS. Teacher leads (models movement and text) while children join in the following fingerplay:

| | |
|---|---|
| Five little polar bears | *Wriggle all five fingers* |
| Playing near the shore | |
| One tumbled in | *Tuck one finger away and* |
| And then there were four | *Hold up four* |
| Four little polar bears | *Wriggle four fingers* |
| Swimming in the sea. | |
| One chased a seal | *Tuck one finger away* |
| And then there were three | *Hold up three* |
| Three little polar bears | |
| What shall we do? | *Etc.* |
| One went swimming | |
| And then there were two. | |
| Two little polar bears | |
| Playing in the sun | |
| One took a nap | |
| And then there was one. | |
| One little polar bear | |
| Not very old | |
| Where's my mom? | |
| I'm hungry and cold. | |

2. BODY OF LESSON. Read *We're Going on a Bear Hunt* without any musical or vocal embellishment—teacher models keeping steady beat (on lap, etc.) during the refrain and vocal sounds on the verses allowing children to move upper bodies (arms) freely while sitting (Note: This goes for most book activities—I have found that young children, especially, need to hear the story at least one time as it is, so they can look at the pictures and take in the story before exploring and experimenting with it).

3. Read the story again. This time the teacher plays sound effects on the drum while children improvise movement for each verse.

4. LESSON EXTENSIONS. Read the story—children play sound effects on drums, hand drums and other instruments

   A. Invite children to join you on a Polar Bear Hike (Note: This is a variation on "Goin' on a Bear Hunt").

      Ready to go on a polar bear hike?
      First, is everyone dressed warmly?

Zip up your snow suit.

Put on your boots.

Pull on your hat.

Wrap your scarf around your neck.

Tuck your hands in your mittens.

Now ... Let's go on a polar bear hike!

*Rub hands on thighs to make a trudging sound as you hike in place.*

Oh, look, we're going through the tundra.

In the summer this would be easy since it is flat and has no trees.

But it's winter now and covered in very deep snow!

Can't go around it. Can't go under it. Have to hike through it.

All right! Let's go!

*Pump arms. Bring knees up as if trudging through deep snow.*

Whew! We made it.

Oh look! I see the Arctic Sea.

Its covered with ice and so cold. Brrr!

Well, can't go around it. Can't go under it. We'll have to skate over it.

All right! Let's go!

*Skating motion*

Look ahead! I see an iceberg.

Can't go around it. Can't go under it. Have to climb over it.

All right! Let's go!

*Climbing motion*

We're almost at the top

Do you see any polar bears?

*Raise hand over eyebrows and look all around.*

Wow! We made it to the top of the iceberg.

Can't walk down. It's much too steep! I know ... let's slide down.

All right! Let's go!

*Slide along on bottoms.*

Oh look! I think I see something over there.

I see a den in the snow.

Can't go around it. Can't go over it. We'll have to crawl in.

All right! Let's go!

*Get down on hands and knees and crawl.*

Oh, it's warmer in here.

You know ... I feel something furry.

Oh no! I think it's a polar bear.

Shhh! Don't wake it.

We're a little too close.

We better get out of here fast!

*Crawl out of the den.*

Let's run

*Running motion.*

Back over the iceberg.

*Climbing motion.*

Slide down the other side

*Slide on bottoms.*

Skate over the Arctic Sea.

*Skating motion.*

Hike through the snowy tundra.

*Lift knees high in place.*

Oh, my! Look!

Do you see what I see?

It's a mother polar bear and her two little cubs coming out of their den for the very first time. Ohhh!

Wow! Now that was worth the hike.

Time to go home!

*Wave goodbye.*

(*CopyCat: Ideas and Activities for K–3 Teachers.* April 2002 )

## Lesson 3 by Julia Church Hoffman

### Book/Literature Selection

*Brown Bear, Brown Bear, What do You See?* by Bill Martin Jr. and Eric Carle

*My Many Colored Days,* by Dr. Seuss

### Early Literacy Goals

Letter knowledge

Print awareness

### Musical Goals

Improvised movement

Playing and exploring percussion instruments

### Materials/Resources Needed

Scarves

Various pitched/unpitched instruments

1. FOCUS. Teacher sings a greeting to each child acknowledging child's name and the color he/she is wearing. Sing to the tune of "The Farmer in the Dell."

> Oh, (name) is wearing blue,
> Oh, (name) is wearing blue.
> High Ho the derry oh,
> (Name) is wearing blue.
> *(Change name and colors accordingly)*

2. BODY OF LESSON. Read *Brown Bear, Brown Bear, What do You See?* Add movement—children select scarves for each color and interpret and move like the animal they select.

3. Add instruments—introduce instruments (woods, metals, drums, etc.)—children determine which instruments they want to portray each color/animal.

4. Color matching game: Teacher holds bag of scarves. She holds up scarves, one by one—each time holding a different color scarf up and sings to individual children. Sing to the tune of "If You're Happy and You Know It."

> If you can name this color sing it loud (Child sings the color of the scarf)
> If you can name this color sing it soft
> If you can name this color and you know it's like no other
> If you can name this color sing it Loud or Soft!

5. LESSON EXTENSION. Read *Brown Bear, Brown Bear, What do You See?* with movement and/or instrumentation.

6. LESSON EXTENSION. The same lesson can be applied to Dr. Seuss' *My Many Colored Days.*

### Lesson 4 by Carla Haynes

#### Book/Literature Selection

*Panda Bear, Panda Bear, What Do You See?* by Bill Martin Jr. and Eric Carle

#### Early Literacy Goals

Phonological awareness

Vocabulary

Narrative skills

#### Musical Goals

Song conversations

Musical questions and answers

Creative movement to vocabulary

### Materials

Assorted stuffed animals (very small so a toddler can hold on lap) or clip art of different animals, one for each child

Basket or container

1. FOCUS. Teacher sings the book using the "Rain Rain Go Away" melody for singing the book—going through page by page.

2. BODY OF LESSON. Show book again, but this time students sing question "Panda Bear, Panda Bear, What Do You See?" The teacher sings the answer. You might want to first invite the entire group to sing the question and later invite one or two children to sing the question.

3. Swap halfway through book so students get used to singing both Q & A. Again, you might want to rely on students who are more comfortable singing alone as the question singers. Show basket (full of stuffed animals/clip art sheets). Pull out one and show students. Teacher sings a question to the animal. "Elephant, Elephant, what do you see?" One by one, students take turns singing questions using the name of animal he/she pulled out. (So the child might sing "kangaroo, kangaroo, what do you see?" Note: Teacher sings A in a solo (singing all alone) by pulling another animal out and using the name and created movement of that animal in the A.

4. All sing Q using that animal's name, teacher sings A in a solo pulling out another animal using the name and created movement of that new animal. Repeat the above in the Q & A game until all the animals have been identified.

5. Students then sit in circle and teacher hands each student an animal. Teacher works around the circle to make sure each child knows what animal/movement they have. Teacher holds an animal up (example: tiger) and the whole class sings "Tiger, Tiger, what do you see?" The person holding the tiger gets to create the movement that a tiger might do. Then the child gets to select another animal choosing one from the circle. For example "I see a bluebird, looking at me."

6. LESSON EXTENSION

    A. After the student sings a solo, their animal goes to sleep behind them. This activity ends naturally and leads to a lullaby.

    B. Students can be seated on one side of a partition while teacher is on the other with instruments. Teacher can sing or chant: "Panda Bear, Panda Bear, what do you *hear*" and play a selected rhythm instrument, challenging the child to identify the instrument through hearing only. The child may answer singing or chanting: "I hear a triangle clanging at me."

**More Books on Bears** (Compiled by Wilma Flanagan)

*Milo's Hat Trick,* by Jon Agee. Hyperion Books for Children, 2001. Milo's magic show is a failure until he meets a bear who knows how to pretend his bones are made of rubber.

*Blackboard Bear*, by Martha Alexander. Candlewick Press, 1999. When a little boy is not allowed to play with the older children, he creates an imaginary friend by drawing a giant bear on his blackboard.

*Every Autumn Comes the Bear,* by Jim Arnosky. Putnam's, 1993. Every autumn a bear shows up behind the farm and goes through a series of routines before finding a den among the hilltop boulders where he sleeps all winter long.

*Where's the Bear?* by Charlotte Pomerantz; pictures by Byron Barton. Greenwillow Books, 1984. A group of townspeople go looking for a bear.

*Sleepy Bear*, by Lydia Dabcovich. Dutton, 1982. Shows Bear getting ready for his long winter's nap, or hibernation, and his springtime awakening.

*Copy Me, Copycub*, by Richard Edwards; pictures by Susan Winter. Harper Collins Publishers, 1999. Copycub, who imitates everything that his mother bear does, follows her to their den when winter comes and snow begins to fall.

*Two Bear Cubs,* by Ann Jonas. Greenwillow Books, 1982. Two adventurous cubs love to wander, but when frightened, appreciate having Mother close by.

*The Bear that Heard Crying,* by Natalie Kinsey-Warnock and Helen Kinsey; pictures by Ted Rand. Cobblehill Books/Dutton, 1993. A fictionalized retelling of the true story of three-year-old Sarah Whitcher, who, in 1783, became lost in the woods of New Hampshire and was protected by a bear until her rescue four days later.

*Blueberries for Sal,* by Robert McCloskey. Viking Press, 1976. Little Sal and her mother, and little bear and his mother get all mixed up among the blueberries of Blueberry Hill one summer day.

*The Bear's Toothache*, by David McPhail. Little, Brown, 1972. When he discovers a bear with a toothache outside his window, a little boy tries to think of ways of removing the tooth.

*Bear,* by John Schoenherr. Philomel Books, 1991. Searching for his mother, a young bear finds his own independence.

*Good Job, Little Bear*, by Martin Waddell; pictures by Barbara Firth. Candlewick, 2002. Little Bear does a good job of climbing rocks, bouncing on a tree branch, and crossing a stream, but Big Bear is always there to lend a helping hand when needed.

*When Will it Be Spring?* by Catherine Walters. Dutton Children's Books, 1998. Although Mother Bear urges Alfie to be patient and sleep, he cannot wait to see tiny butterflies on the wing and hear baby birds chirp in the trees.

*The Biggest Bear,* by Lynd Ward. Houghton Mifflin, 1952. Johnny goes hunting for a bear-skin to hang on his family's barn and returns with a small bundle of trouble.

## GROUP B: A NATURE WALK

### Lesson 5 by Carla Haynes

*Book/Literature Selection*

*The Listening Walk*, by Paul Showers; illustrated by Aliki

*Early Literacy Goals*

Print awareness and vocabulary

*Musical Goals*

Listening

Describing tone color

Starting and stopping

*Materials*

Drawing area (dry erase board, chalk board, large pad of paper)

Drawing instrument (pen, marker, chalk)

Conductor's baton or pointer or mallet

1. FOCUS. Teacher invites children to close eyes and listen for sounds the room is making (ambient sounds). Teacher asks children to name and describe the sounds heard. Teacher shows the cover of book *The Listening Walk* and discusses the title with children.

2. BODY OF LESSON. Prepare children for the book by drawing attention to the sound words in the book (the jet noise is *eeeyyyyooooowwwwooo*). Read it through with vocal inflections on the sound words. Teacher encourages children to join in on the sound words.

3. Invite children to go on a "listening walk" around the building or center. (The walk should be *very* short and not too far away from the room.) The rules for the listening walk:

   • Try to be quiet in your feet and mouth.
   • Use your ears to listen for sounds.
   • Try to remember as many sounds as you can.

4. After the walk, the teacher encourages the students to share the sound noises they heard.

5. The teacher draws those sounds (a simple pictorial representation or an icon will be fine) on the board one at a time, inviting children to experiment with vocal sounds. Each time the teacher draws a sound (do not draw more than six sounds), the children pick and choose ones to practice.

6. After the icons are established so they are meaningful to the children, and they have practiced them, the teacher becomes the "conductor" and using the conductor's baton, points to various sound pictures and invites children to perform the sound.

7. When the baton touches a sound picture, children begin to vocalize that sound and continue the sound as long as the baton points to the icon. Once the baton is lifted off of the sound picture, students stop the sound. Teacher continues to touch each sound picture (with various durations) until students master starting and stopping their vocalization with the placement of the baton.

8. Teacher then hands the baton to a student and that student becomes the conductor. Each student should have the opportunity to be the conductor.

9. LESSON EXTENSIONS

   A. Create a sound composition with the individual sounds chosen.
   B. Identify sounds of animals and play the conductor game with those sounds.
   C. Choose body percussion/nonpitched instruments instead of vocalization.

**More Books on Autumn and Nature** (Compiled by Wilma Flanagan)

*Every Autumn Comes the Bear,* by Jim Arnosky. Putnam's, 1993. Every autumn a bear shows up behind the farm and goes through a series of routines before finding a den among the hilltop boulders where he sleeps all winter long.

*Red Leaf, Yellow Leaf,* by Lois Ehlert. Harcourt Brace Jovanovich, 1991. A child describes the growth of a maple tree from seed to sapling.

*Time to Sleep,* by Denise Fleming. Holt, 1997. When Bear notices that winter is nearly here he hurries to tell Snail, after which each animal tells another until finally the already sleeping Bear is awakened in his den with the news.

*Fall Leaves Fall!* by Zoe Hall; illustrated by Shari Halpern. Scholastic Press, 2000. When fall comes, two brothers enjoy catching the falling leaves, stomping on them, kicking them, jumping in piles of them and using them to make pictures. Includes a description of how leaves change through the year.

*Wild Child,* by Lynn Plourde; illustrated by Greg Couch. Simon & Schuster Books for Young Readers, 1999. Mother Earth attempts to put her wild child, Autumn, to bed.

*Winter Lullaby* by Barbara Seuling; illustrated by Greg Newbold. Browndeer Press, Harcourt Brace, 1998. Depicts the ways various animals spend the cold months of winter, from bats sleeping in caverns to fish swimming deeper in lakes where the water is warmer.

*The Stranger,* by Chris Van Allsburg. Houghton Mifflin, 1986. The enigmatic origins of the stranger Farmer Bailey hits with his truck and brings home to recuperate seem to have a mysterious relation to the changing season.

## Lesson 6 by Carla Haynes: Ladybugs!

### Book/Literature Selection

*The Very Lazy Ladybug,* by Isobel Finn and Jack Tickly

### Early Literacy Goals

Vocabulary

Phonological awareness

Print awareness

### Musical Goals

Singing

Performing a chant

Playing instruments

### Materials

Ladybug hand puppet

Hand drum for each child

Seven different animal icons with action word printed (all from book)

- Kangaroo—Jump
- Lion—Roar
- Crocodile—Swish
- Monkey—Swing
- Bear—Scratch
- Turtle—Snooze
- Elephant—Sneezed

1. FOCUS. Teacher shows ladybug puppet. Greets each child individually and sings "Hello" with puppet. Child sings solo back, "Hello."
2. Teacher presents cover of book and discuss ladybugs. This book is about a lazy one— discuss.

3. BODY OF LESSON. Teacher reads book.

4. Teacher and children discuss the different animals in the book and their actions and movements.

5. As the discussion is going on, the teacher shows each icon individually and invites the children to create a movement associated with each card.

6. Teacher shares song while patting a steady beat. (This can be also be done as a chant.) Chant: "The very lazy ladybug wished she could fly. She met with a _____ and all he did was _____." Teach song while keeping a steady beat. Sing song for each card.

7. The teacher distributes hand drums to all children singing (or chanting) while keeping a steady beat on hand drum with fingertips.

8. Teacher inserts different animals (mentioned above) and their actions into song/chant and performs differing actions on the drum head. Example: Jump—bounce fingers up and down on head of drum. Roar—roll fingertips at a fast pace on the head of drum. Scratch—use fingernails and scratch head of drum. Perform each card in sequence to the book with song (keeping steady beat in drum), and finger movements.

9. LESSON EXTENSION. Assign each animal to a child. Act out the book using ladybug hand puppet and child animal actors. (All other students are singing/chanting melody and playing hand drums.)

## Lesson 7 by Carla Haynes: More Ladybugs!

### Book/Literature Selection

*Ten Little Ladybugs,* by Melanie Gerth; illustrated by Laura Huliska-Beith

### Early Literacy Skills

Counting

Phonological awareness

Print awareness

*Musical Goal*

Chanting to a steady beat

Singing

*Materials*

Ten ladybug icons

Six different animal icons representing characters in book. Possibilities: Butterfly, Caterpillar, Duck, Frog, Grasshopper, Fish, Bird, Bee, Turtle, Wind

1. FOCUS. Teacher chants this fingerplay with children.

> Five little ladybugs climbing up a door
> One flew away and then there were four.
> Four little ladybugs climbing up a tree
> One flew away and then there were three
> Three little ladybugs landed on a shoe
> One flew away and then there were two.
> Two little ladybugs look for some fun,
> One flew away and then there was one.
> One little lady sitting in the sun,
> She flew away and then there were none.

2. BODY OF LESSON. Teacher chants one to ten in steady beat with students. Teacher asks, "Where can we keep a steady beat on our body while counting?" Students create place to keep steady beat while counting (on legs, on head, clapping, etc.). Perform child created steady beat while counting one to ten each time. Teacher shows book. Discuss ladybugs on cover, count them, etc. Teacher reads the book to children, chanting the poem, using inflections and gestures to dramatize the story emphasizing the countdown. Discuss animals that appeared in the book. Show icons of each animal and distribute to ten individual students.

3. Show ten ladybug icons and distribute to ten different students.

4. Students with animal icons (not ladybugs) stand on one side of the room. Students with ladybug icons stand on the other side of the room. Teacher shows and sings the book as the class acts out the book. Example: "Ten little ladybugs sitting on a vine" (students with ladybugs pretend to sit on a vine), "Along came a butterfly—" (Pause while the student with the butterfly icon flys over and chooses a student with a ladybug and they both fly and sit down), "Then there were nine." Continue the process until there is one ladybug and when the class sings "Then she was home," all the sitting animals and ladybugs join the last standing ladybug.

## GROUP C: JUMPING JACKS AND MONKEYS

### Lesson 8 by Carla Haynes: Five Little Monkeys

*Book/Literature Selection*

*Five Little Monkeys Jumping on the Bed,* by Eileen Christelow

*Early Literacy Goals*

Counting

Phonological awareness

*Musical Goals*

Steady beat

Chant-speaking voice

Playing instruments

*Materials*

Brown paper bag

Five monkey finger puppets or clip art cut-outs or small stuffed animal monkeys

Five large hand drums

1. FOCUS. Teacher shows children a brown paper bag and leads discussion of what might be hiding in the bag.
2. Teacher introduces monkey finger puppets one at a time, making sure to encourage children to keep track of how many there are. (There will be five!)
3. When all five monkeys are out of the bag, teacher tells children that they will be reading a book about five little monkeys who love to play together.
4. BODY OF LESSON. Teacher introduces book and leads discussion of illustration on the front cover.
5. The teacher reads the book, chanting while keeping a steady beat.
6. The teacher reads the book again, inviting students to chant along.
7. The teacher shows one large circular hand drum and introduces the drum as the monkey's bed. Teacher makes the monkey "jump on the bed" by placing the finger puppet in the

center of the drum head and tapping on the rim to make the monkey "jump." Teacher continues the chant until "one fell off and bumped his head" and removes the monkey from the "bed." Teacher pantomimes "Mama called the doctor and the doctor said. 'No more monkeys jumping on the bed!'"

8. Teacher distributes four large hand drums and places a monkey puppet on each and children as a group make the monkey "jump on the bed" as they tap the steady beat to the chant.

## Lesson 9 by Julia Church Hoffman: Bling Blang

### Book/Literature Selection

*Bling Blang,* by Woody Guthrie, pictures by Vladimir Radunsky (comes with a CD)

### Early Literacy Goals

Phonological awareness

Print awareness

### Musical Goals

Perform steady beat

### Materials/Resources Needed

A set of tools for demonstration

1. FOCUS. Start with song "Johnny Works with One Hammer" (See Appendix B). (You may also chant the words and tap or clap on the X if you feel more comfortable)

```
     X    X       X  X
     Johnny Works with One Hammer,
     X  X       X  X
     One Hammer, One Hammer
     X    X       X  X
     Johnny Works with One Hammer,
     X   X  X        X
     Then He Works with Two _____.
```

Johnny works with two hammers, then he works with three. The song continues to five hammers, then Johnny goes on strike!

2. BODY OF LESSON. Children are seated around teacher, who is asking question about the different tools.

3. Discuss tools and the jobs they perform.

4. Teacher invites children to describe the sound of tools (inspired by Paula Diekoff). Then you can ask the children to help you make up a song about tool sounds, using "Wheels on the Bus." Some suggested ideas for tool sounds: "The hammer in the shop goes bang, bang, bang!" "The drill in the shop goes br-r-r, br-r-r, br-r-r." "The saw in the shop goes buzz, buzz, buzz."

5. Show the book *Bling Blang* and play the recording.

6. On chorus—hammer the beat for "bling blang" and saw for "zingo-zango"—try creating a new motion with a partner or two.

7. Teacher invites children to draw pictures of a house they would like to build.

**Lesson 10 by Julia Church Hoffman: Complainin' Jack**

*Age or Grade Level*

Preschool

*Book/Literature Selection*

"Complainin' Jack," from *Falling Up,* by Shel Silverstein

*Integrated Content Objective*

Rhyming words

*Fine Arts/Musical Objective*

Choral reading—different voices

Improvised movement

Nonlocomotor movement

Solo singing

*Materials/Resources Needed*

"Toy Shop," from *Highlighting the Holidays* by Jeff Kriske and Randy DeLelles

Multicolored scarves, one for each child

Colored construction paper (with as many different colors as the scarves)

1. FOCUS. Recite "Toy Shop" chant with steady beat (on lap, or somewhere)—talk about toys, act out children's favorite toys in the B section—make sure one is a jack-in-the-box.

| | |
|---|---|
| Toy shop Toy shop | *Beat keeping* |
| Let's go to the toy shop | |
| Peek inside, eyes are wide | *peek eyes, show wide eyes* |
| Show us what you see . . . | *put hands out to show something* |

2. Then kids pantomime what they see in a toy shop. Teacher leads pantomime and says, "I see an airplane," then kids pantomime an airplane. Then kids pantomime toys and children. Then do chant again—and do another toy.

3. Read Shel Silverstein's "Complainin' Jack." Ask about all the things Jack complained about (crack, tack, snack, quack), *all* rhyme with "Jack."

4. For older children, instruct children to listen for "How many voices are in this poem?" (two—narrator and Jack)

5. Repeat poem a number of times so that children begin to absorb it. Throughout the repetition, you might want to

   • Invite children to help create motions for the poem

   • As a group or individually, invite children to create a visual for the poem

6. Teacher says to children "We each get to be a jack-in -the-box." Teacher passes out multicolored scarves, then models and invites children to sit on their knees and tell them to "jump out of the box" when I call out their color.

7. LESSON EXTENSION. Use a favorite instrumental recording as a sound carpet and background music and teacher holds up a piece of construction paper to match one of the colors of the scarves and the child "jumps" out of the box when his/her color appears.

**More Books on Toys** (Compiled by Wilma Flanagan)

*Lisa Cannot Sleep*, by Kaj Beckman; pictures by Per Beckman. F. Watts, 1970. A little girl who can't sleep without her doll ends up with so many toys in bed that there is no room for her.

*Just Like Jasper!* by Nick Butterworth and Mick Inkpen. Little, Brown, 1989. Jasper Cat goes to a toy store to spend his birthday money.

*Ten Little Animals*, by Laura Jane Coats. Macmillan, 1990. A counting book in which one by one ten little animals jump on the bed, only to fall off and bump their heads.

*Ten Play Hide-and-Seek,* by Penny Dale. Candlewick Press, 1998. A little boy and nine stuffed animals play hide and seek before going to bed.

*Tidy Titch,* by Pat Hutchins. Greenwillow Books, 1991. Titch helps his older brother and sister clean their rooms.

*The Blue Balloon,* by Mick Inkpen. Little, Brown, 1990. A child (with the help of artful pull-out pages) explains the extraordinary features of his blue balloon.

*The Steadfast Tin Soldier,* retold and illustrated by Rachel Isadora. Putnam's Sons, 1996. The perilous adventures of a toy soldier who loves a paper dancing girl culminate in tragedy for both of them.

*Now We Can Go,* by Ann Jonas. Greenwillow Books, 1986. A child must take all the toys from her toy box and put them in her bag before she is ready to go.

*Where Can it Be?* by Ann Jonas. Greenwillow Books, 1986. A child looks all over the house for her missing blanket. Uses flaps to reveal what the child finds behind closed doors.

*The Marvelous Toy,* by Tom Paxton; illustrated by Elizabeth Sayles. Morrow Junior Books, 1996. A father gives to his young son the same marvelous toy that his father had given to him many years before.

*The Little Engine That Could*, retold by Watty Piper; illustrated by George and Doris Hauman. Platt & Munk, 1961. When the other engines refuse, the Little Blue Engine tries to pull a stranded train full of dolls, toys and good food over the mountain.

*On Top of the World*, by John Prater. Mondo, 1998. On a warm night in a moonlit playground, four toy animals climb and climb to the top of the world and then have the fun of coming down again.

*The Line Up Book*, by Marisabina Russo. Greenwillow Books, 1986. Sam lines up blocks, books, boots, cars and other objects, all the way from his room to his mother in the kitchen.

*Block City*, by Robert Louis Stevenson; illustrated by Ashley Wolff. E. P. Dutton, 1988. A child creates a world of his own which has mountains and sea, a city and ships, all from toy blocks.

*Good Night, Everyone!* by Harriet Ziefert; illustrated by Andrea Baruffi. Boston: Little, Brown, 1988. A tired Harry wants to sleep but his toys decide to play noisily.

## REFERENCES

Andress, Barbara. *Music for Young Children.* Fort Worth: Harcourt Brace College Publishers, 1998.
Brett, Jan. *Berlioz the Bear.* New York: Putnam Juvenile, 1999.
Carle, Eric. *Papa, Please Get the Moon for Me.* New York: Simon and Schuster, 1986.
Christelow, Eileen. *Five Little Monkeys Jumping on the Bed.* New York: Clarion Books, 1998.
Ehlert, Lois. *Leaf Man.* New York: Harcourt Children's Books, 1998.
Finn, Isobel, and Jack Tickly. *The Very Lazy Ladybug.* Wilton, CT: Tiger Tales, 2003.

Fleming, Denise. *Barnyard Banter.* New York: Holt, 1994.

Fleming, Denise. *In the Tall Tall Grass.* New York: Holt, 1991.

Fox, Mem, and Jane Dyer. *Time for Bed.* New York: Red Wagon Books, 1997.

Franco, Betsey, and Shari Halpern. *Fresh Fall Leaves.* New York: Scholastic, 1994.

Ghigna, Charles. *Animal Trunk: Silly Poems to Read Aloud.* New York: Harry N. Abrams, 1999.

Guthrie, Woody. *Bling Blang.* Cambridge, MA: Candlewick Press, 2000.

Inkpen, Mick. *Lullabyhullaballoo.* London: Hodden Children's Books, 1995.

Kalan, Robert, and Byron Barton. *Jump Frog Jump!* New York: William Morrow, 1981.

Long, Sylvia. *Hush Little Baby.* New York: Scholastic, 1997.

Martin, Bill, Jr., and Eric Carle. *Brown Bear, Brown Bear, What Do You See?* New York: Holt, 1995.

Martin, Bill, Jr., and Eric Carle. *Polar Bear, Polar Bear, What Do You Hear?* New York: Holt, 1991.

McDonald, Dorothy. *Music in Our Lives: The Early Years.* Washington, DC: National Association for the Education of Young Children, 1979.

Rosen, Michael, and Helen Oxenbury. *We're Goin' on a Bear Hunt.* New York: Little Simon, 1997.

Seuss, Dr. *My Many Colored Days.* New York: Knopf Books for Young Readers, 1996.

Silverstein, Shel. *Falling Up.* New York: Harper Collins, 1996.

Showers, Paul, and Aliki. *The Listening Walk.* New York: Harper Trophy, 1993.

Wise, Margaret Brown, and Clement Hurd. *Good Night Moon.* New York: Harper Festival, 1991.

# CHAPTER 5

## *The Primary Grades: K–2*

Because of the influence of the proponents of Developmentally Appropriate Practice, and others who have advocated for study of early childhood, children in the primary grades (K–2) have an opportunity to play and learn in school in ways that respond to their level of growth. While it is clear that all children do not develop at the same rate, this chapter is based on general expectations for musical and creative possibilities for children in the early elementary school grades. It is my hope that these benchmarks will serve as a point of reference for teachers, librarians and childcare providers for lesson and story time planning.

Children in the primary grades are beginning to have more gross and fine motor control and are able to sit longer than preschool-aged children. Rules in games in the classroom and at home become increasingly important at this time, as well as the concepts of cooperation and competition. Logical thought process is beginning to emerge by the beginning of second grade and so, by then, most children are able to use written symbols to convey meaning and represent spoken language.

With these developmental ideas in place, it is logical to expect that:

- children will have many opportunities to sing, chant, move and play instruments alone and with others;
- children will be able to discuss and differentiate instruments and voices that make different kinds of sounds;
- directed musical listening experiences in lesson plans and story times should be included as often as possible; and
- opportunities for creativity and improvisation should be presented frequently.

The following narrative describes one teacher's approach to help her students make connections via their need to use language to initiate physical action and to begin to explain these actions in greater detail. In this narrative, the teacher uses a rhythmic chant and a game involving steady beat to stress consistency, creativity and structure.

### Move Like a Clown

The first graders in Mrs. Whorley's class at Joe Lewis elementary school are sitting in their classroom after lunch. Their teacher asks the children to make up some motions for a game they will play. She invites individual children to perform motions and challenges the rest of the class to describe the motions and write the words on the chalkboard. The words they come up with are:

Shake

Twirl

Run in place

Twist

Rub

Nod

Next she invites the children to sit in a circle, and she teaches them a rhythmic chant. The children learn it quickly and their voices take on this lively rhythmic taunt as they keep a steady beat on their lap:

> The clown got sick!
> The clown got sick!

The teacher, also keeping a beat questions the class—pointing to one student: "How did the clown get sick?"

That student responds demonstrating a motion—rubbing his belly—while the class imitates the student leader. "The clown got sick from doing this!" The class chants while continuing the motion

> The clown got sick!
> The clown got sick!

The teacher again questions another student: "How did the clown get sick?"

The class continues to chant rhythmically and imitate student leaders until Mrs. Whorley says, "I have a book about the adventures of Clown—there are no words in this book but it tells a story about Clown and some decisions he makes. Can you help me tell the story with words?" Mrs. Whorley gathers the children around her and begins to read the story "Clown" by Quentin Blake.

## SINGING IN THE PRIMARY GRADES

By now, most children are able to differentiate between singing, shouting and speaking. They are able to sway, pat and step while they sing and can begin to play simple instruments while singing. Because children at this age need to express thought through action, singing games and story songs are developmentally appropriate and provide a great release as well. Dramatic play and a way of physically expressing fantasy are often wonderful outlets for children in grades K–2.

Songs can be acted out—especially story songs. Children love singing along with a book or hearing a story sung. For kindergarten children, a beautifully illustrated story of a simple familiar song allows five-year-olds a chance to act out a known story with a surprise ending, thus allowing children to use movement and singing as an avenue to express what they know as well as to create something different. The book *The Itsy Bitsy Spider* by Iza Trapini is based on a familiar tune coupled with old and new words and offers such a challenge:

> The itsy bitsy spider
> Climbed up the kitchen wall.
> Swoosh! went the fan
> And made the spider fall.
> Off went the fan.
> No longer did it blow.
> So the itsy bitsy spider
> Back up the wall did go.

*The **Ballad** of Valentine* by Alison Jackson is a humorous story set to the tune "My Darling Clementine" that describes a mountain woman and her harried suitor's disastrous attempts to connect through love letters. First- and second-grade children will enjoy adding motions, gestures or pantomime to this story. A similar tale is the book *She'll Be Comin' Round the Mountain,* adapted by Tom Birdseye and Debbie Holsclaw Birdseye. Older second graders will enjoy the extension of this familiar tune through an engaging story that describes relationships with family and friends in detail.

**Singing games** are an important part of social development in the primary grades. Game songs like *Doggie Doggie Where's Your Bone* will easily connect with stories like John Grogan's *Bad Dog, Marley!* or *Fun Dog, Sun Dog* by Deborah Heiligman. In this hiding game, children love to disguise their voices as they hide the stolen bone from the poor doggie.

> GROUP: Doggie doggie, where's your bone? Somebody's stole it from your home.
> DOGGIE: Who has my bone?
> ONE CHILD: Woof! Woof! Woof!

1. One child is the doggie—who sits blindfolded with his back to the class with his "bone" behind him.
2. While the class sings the first two lines, one person from the group quietly sneaks up and takes the bone, and hides it behind his/her back.
3. When the DOGGIE sings "Who has my bone?" the child who has taken the bone responds with a *Woof Woof Woof* in a disguised voice.
4. The DOGGIE child has three tries to guess who stole the bone.

Because primary age children are developing an increased ability to memorize words, it is a good idea to create a list of known songs that children can sing together. Sometimes this tune bank can be used to create new songs based on text from a story capitalizing on most children's natural instincts to want to sing.

## RHYTHMIC CHANTING AND CLAPPING

By the time children begin kindergarten they can usually tap along with a regular pulse or steady beat. I find that chanting on beat is easy for children—and patting along on laps, knees or the floor helps keep everyone together. It is always easier to invite children to pat the beat on their laps at first—as some children have a difficult time with the coordination of beat matching while clapping. For some children there are too many variables in the distance between the span of two outstretched hands.

Short poems are a fine way to help five- and six-year-old children learn to chant together. The chanting game *Who Stole the Cookie from the Cookie Jar?* is combined with a counting-in-reverse poem in the book by Margaret Wang. This clever story gives children an opportunity to anticipate rhyming words while chanting to a steady beat.

> I was playing in the den
> When I noticed there were ten.
> Oh it's such a pity!
> It must have been the _____ [turn the next page to find the word *kitty*]

In the echoing chant *I Have a Cat,* children echo the teacher while keeping a steady beat either by tapping or clapping.

| | |
|---|---|
| TEACHER: I have a cat. | CHILDREN echo |
| TEACHER: My cat is fat. | CHILDREN echo |

TEACHER: I have a cat.             CHILDREN echo
TEACHER: My cat wears a hat.       CHILDREN echo
TEACHER: My cat caught a bat!      CHILDREN echo
TEACHER: I have a cat.             CHILDREN echo
ALL: MEEEEEEOOOOOOOW!

There are many variations to use with this chant. For example, tapping the beat while the teacher speaks and gestures as the whole class echoes. Sometimes, rhythm instruments can be used to tell the story—or use a specific instrument when the word "cat" is mentioned.

## USING RECORDINGS WITH K–2

In order to have successful experience using recordings with children in the primary grades, it is important to make sure that we treat music listening as a skill that can be developed. When we ask children to listen to a recording or use it to enhance a book or a story we have to find ways to creatively engage children. In order to do that, we ourselves must know why we're using the recording. Likewise, listening activities should be multi-sensory, involving the kinesthetic, visual as well as aural senses.

Kindergarten children usually have longer attention spans than do preschool children and are generally more accustomed to sitting quietly. In my work as a music teacher, I have found that even kindergarten children will be able to sit and listen to live performances much more readily than hearing a recording. So if I am going to use a recording with children that involves a solo instrument, if possible I invite a guest artist to play for my class beforehand. I find that because they have already seen and heard the instrument live, when I use a recording, they can generally do the activity or listen to the story without being quite so distracted by the instrument itself. Sometimes, when a guest artist is not available, I have taken photographs of the instrument being played by someone—and lead a discussion about the instrument and the performer in the photograph before I go onto the lesson.

There are many **story recordings**—one of the most famous is Prokofiev's *Peter and the Wolf*. There are countless recordings of this story—usually narrated by a prominent actor and accompanied by a full orchestra. The musical themes are easily identifiable and first and second graders will enjoy acting out the story as the recording goes on. (See Appendix C.) Camille Saint-Saëns's *Carnival of the Animals*—a set of orchestral character pieces just over twenty-two minutes long—has been adapted to a children's book. The book *Carnival of the Animals* by Barrie C. Turner features a commentary about each of each of the pieces as well as a music-only recording. This children's book makes the orchestral masterwork of Saint-Saëns completely accessible to children in grades K–2.

There is also an endless selection of vocal recordings for use with children grades K–2. Many songs in different genres are appropriate to use to help make connections across the elementary curriculum. I find that listening to folk songs from the United States and from around the world help children understand about their own cultures and ones that are different from their own.

## MOVING PLAYFULLY

Children in the primary grades are beginning to develop skipping, galloping and jump rope skills. They can participate in folk dances that require circle and line formation. Skipping is usually a more complicated skill and once they have mastered galloping, trotting and hopping, children are ready to skip in dances and circle games.

Action songs and games are an important part of the daily life of children in elementary school—especially in the primary grades. The game "Aunt Dinah's Gone" is a wonderful example of a call-and-response game that gives children (and the teacher) an opportunity to respond creatively and playfully to a rhyme.

> Aunt Dinah's gone. [Echo]
> Well how did she leave? [Echo]
> Well she left like this. [Echo]
>
> Chorus:
> She lives in the country
> Gonna move to town
> Gonna shake and shimmy
> 'Til the sun goes down.

This chant is done in a call-response manner. On the line "Well she left like this," the leader strikes a pose that the rest of the group imitates. On the next line, the leader changes poses, and the group follows. All join in on the chorus. On the line "Gonna shake and shimmy," the leader moves according to his or her idea of what that means. Substitute the leader's name for Aunt Dinah, using "Uncle" when appropriate.

Once they are able to keep with the beat of the music, children in the primary grades can usually begin to have success participating in simple folk dances. Exposing children to the world of folk dance is a way to help young children understand the activities of people from various cultures and the spirit of how these activities were carried out. While dancing in the classroom, library or living room might take a little extra planning, it is both an art form and a form of recreation that can enliven a child's connection to his or her world by telling a story, creating a mood or expressing an emotion.

It is important to make room for dance and movement activities by moving furniture or equipment. If you are confined to a smaller space, find creative ways to use that space. I sometimes create movements for a story by building a dance out of nonlocomotor hand and arm movements. Creative movement can be inspired by a picture in a book, a poem, a repeated line of text or a piece of music. I use the book *Rap a Tap Tap: Here's Bojangles—Think of That!* to allow children to create a movement for the recurring phrase "rap a tap tap—think of that!"

## PLAYING INSTRUMENTS

While children ages five to seven are beginning to develop gross motor movements, their fine motor coordination is increasing as well. As they grow in strength, agility and flexibility, so too is their ability to play the drum and other rhythm instruments. It is usually a good idea to prepare students for playing instruments by giving opportunity to practice the motor coordination without the instrument in hand. *Rap a Tap Tap* is a good book to use for an introduction to rhythm instruments. I have allowed the children to freely experiment with possibilities on the recurring passages in the first read-through of a story. On the second read-through of the book, I'll ask for more synchronized "drumming" or tapping.

A side note: Many parents and teachers wonder about the right age at which to start a child on a solo instrument such as piano, drums or guitar. While there is no definitive answer to this question, I believe that it if a child sings well, can keep a steady beat on a rhythm instrument and can begin to pick out small melodies on a piano or guitar, then he is ready to begin solo lessons. For some children this can be as young as age five, and for some, it is not until eight or nine years of age. What is key in this equation is the development of the child and his or her prior musical experiences. Piano or drum lessons are not the best entry point for a child who has no prior musical experiences. By and large, the best early musical experiences in the primary grades involve playful exploration with rhythm instruments, many opportunities to sing and create songs and an abundance of joyful child-centered rhymes, poems and chants.

## LESSON IDEAS FOR GRADES K–2

The following lesson ideas are based on lesson plans contributed by Jan Delgado, Carla Haynes, Julia Church Hoffman and Kay Martin.

### Lesson 1 by Kay Martin: Rain Dances

This is a lesson that involves the creation of a thunderstorm using **body percussion** and **rhythm instruments.** This lesson introduces a number of short poems about rain.

#### Grade

1st or 2nd grade

#### Book/Literature Selection

*Listen to the Rain,* by Bill Martin Jr. and John Archambault

#### Language Arts Activity

Create an original poem

#### Musical Activity

Create a **rhythm sound piece** using differing dynamics
Create new **musical form** using rhythm sound piece

#### Materials/Resources

Chant: *Rain on the Green Grass*
Various "rain" poems
Sand blocks, rainsticks, triangles, finger cymbals, rhythm sticks and drums

1. FOCUS. Students and teacher pat a steady beat as they learn the following rhyme:

> Rain on the green grass,
> And rain on the sea,
> Rain on the house-tops,
> But not on me.

2. BODY OF LESSON. Discuss the cycle of a thunderstorm.

3. Create a rainstorm—Create thunderstorm drawing attention to the Italian **expressive terms** (in italics below) and their English translation.

   a. Rub hands together—*piano* = softly
   b. Snap fingers—*mezzo piano* = medium soft
   c. Pat hands on legs—*mezzo forte* = medium loud
   d. Stomp feet on ground/play drums—*forte* = loud
   e. Pat hands on legs—*mezzo forte* = medium loud
   f. Snap fingers—*mezzo piano* = medium soft
   g. Rub hands together, stop—*piano* = soft

4. Read the book *Listen to the Rain* through once, inviting children to notice how the rainstorm comes and goes in the book. Discuss how you might accompany the book with a body percussion rainstorm. Encourage the children to use the Italian expressive terms to convey the loudness and softness appropriate to the book.

5. Add rainstorm accompaniment to a second reading of the book.

6. Create a rainstorm using rhythm instruments, noting which instruments will create the desired effect.

7. LESSON EXTENSION. Put students into small groups and invite them to come up with sound pieces using both body percussion and rhythm instruments to accompany the following chants. (Note: You also might want to encourage students to create their own poetry about rain and thunderstorms.)

   **It's Raining, It's Pouring**
   It's raining, it's pouring,
   The old man is snoring.
   He bumped his head, and he went to bed,
   And he couldn't get up in the morning.

   **The Rain**
   Pitter-patter, raindrops,
   Falling from the sky;
   Here is my umbrella
   To keep me safe and dry!
   When the rain is over,
   And the sun begins to glow,
   Little flowers start to bud,
   And grow and grow and grow!

   **Thunder Crashes**
   Thunder crashes.
   Lightning flashes.

Rain makes puddles,
I make splashes.

### Raindrops

Raindrops are such funny things.
They haven't feet or haven't wings.
Yet they sail through the air,
With the greatest of ease,
And dance on the street,
Wherever they please.

**More Books on Rain** (Compiled by Wilma Flanagan)

*Mr. Gumpy's Motor Car,* by John Burningham. Crowell, 1976. Mr. Gumpy's human and animal friends squash into his old car and go for a drive—until it starts to rain.

*Jack—It's a Rainy Day,* by Rebecca Elgar. Kingfisher, 1999. A lift-the-flap pull-the-tab book on board pages.

*Mushroom in the Rain,* adapted from the Russian of V. Suteyev, by Mirra Ginsburg; pictures by Jose Aruego and Ariane Dewey. Macmillan, 1974. How can an ant, butterfly, mouse, sparrow and rabbit all take shelter from the rain under the same mushroom when originally there was room only for the ant?

*In the Rain with Baby Duck,* by Amy Hest; illustrated by Jill Barton. Candlewick Press, 1995. Although her parents love walking in the rain, Baby Duck does not—until Grandpa shares a secret with her.

*Amy Loves the Rain,* by Julia Hoban; pictures by Lillian Hoban. Harper and Row, 1989. Amy and her mother drive through the rain to pick up Daddy.

*Rain,* by Robert Kalan; illustrated by Donald Crews. Greenwillow Books, 1978. Brief text and illustrations describe a rainstorm.

*Hello, Goodbye*, by David Lloyd; illustrated by Louise Voce. Lothrop, Lee and Shepard Books, 1988. A bear, two bees, some birds and other creatures meet at a tree and say hello until the rain begins and they say goodbye.

*Puddles,* by Jonathan London; pictures by G. Brian Karas. Viking, 1997. When the rain stops falling and the skies clear up, it's time to put on boots and go outside to play in the puddles.

*The Rainy Day Puddle*, by Ei Nakaeayashi. Random House, 1989. Little Frog's puddle grows bigger on a rainy day but becomes much more crowded as other animals come to join him.

*Pete's Puddles*, by Hannah Roche; illustrated by Pierre Pratt. De Agostini Editions, 1996. When it's rainy, Pete can't play outside, but when it stops, he loves to splash around in the puddles.

*The Rain Came Down*, by David Shannon. Blue Sky Press, 2000. An unexpected rain shower causes quarreling among the members of a small community.

*Wet World,* by Norma Simon; illustrated by Alexi Natchev. Candlewick Press, 1995. Describes a little girl's activities on a wet, wet, wet day.

*Rain*, by Manya Stojic. Crown, 2000. The animals of the African savanna use their senses to predict and then enjoy the rain.

*In the Middle of the Puddle,* by Mike Thaler; pictures by Bruce Degen. Harper and Row, 1988. A frog and a turtle watch the rain turn their puddle into an ocean before the sun comes along and returns things to normal.

### *Poetry About Rain*

*Rainy Day Rhymes,* selected by Gail Radley; illustrated by Ellen Kandoian. Houghton Mifflin, 1992. A collection of poems about rainy days and nights, by authors including Elizabeth Coatsworth, Myra Cohn Livingston and Aileen Fisher.

*Rainy Day: Stories and Poems,* edited by Caroline Feller Bauer; illustrated by Michele Chessare. HarperCollins, 1985. A collection of stories and poems about rain by a variety of authors.

### Lesson 2 by Carla Haynes: Poetry in Motion

This lesson encourages children to experiment combining **call and response** and improvised movements as well as an opportunity to create original poetry.

### *Grade*

Kindergarten or 1st Grade

### *Book/Literature Selection*

*From Head to Toe,* by Eric Carle

### *Language Arts Activity*

Create short poems based on repeated text

### *Musical Activity*

Simple chant, movement

## Materials

Six drums or other beat-keeping instrument

Six different animal icons: Example: Butterfly, Frog, Chicken, Dinosaur, Lion, Fish

1. FOCUS. Teacher plays mirror game, inviting children to imitate movements in tandem stressing head, shoulders and upper body parts.

2. Teacher challenges students to echo and touch, improvising a chant

   Teacher: Head Head Head Chin    Students: Head Head Head Chin

   Teacher: Nose Nose Head Ears    Students: Nose Nose Head Ears

   Teacher: Ears -------Ears-------    Students: Ears------- Ears-------

3. BODY OF LESSON. Teacher reads book, inviting students to discuss animals in book. Leads students to practice movements described in book.

4. Read book again with students adding particular movement at appropriate times.

5. Divide students into six groups. Each group is given one animal icon and one drum. Each group identifies the animal by name and creates a movement for it. After the movement is created and practiced students work their movement into the following chant accompanied by a steady beat chanting "I am a [animal name], And I can [movement]. Can *you* do it?" The group counts 1 2 3 4 5 6 7 8, while the rest of the class performs their motion.

6. After the movement game children (either in groups or individually) are given chart paper and asked to come up with a four line poem about their animal.

7. LESSON EXTENSION. Groups (or individuals) read their poems while the rest of the class keeps steady beat.

### Lesson 3 by Julia Church Hoffman: A Chorus of Whales

This lesson is based on the wonders of ocean life and encourages children to move expressively to the sound of whales. Children and teacher will have an opportunity to explore instruments that sound like the ocean.

## Grade

1st or 2nd

## Book/Literature Selection

*The Whale's Song*, by Dyan Sheldon; paintings by Gary Blythe

*The Rainbow Fish*, by Mark Pfister

*Chorus of Whales: Relaxing Sounds of Nature* (CD)

*John Denver's Ancient Rhymes: A Dolphin Lullaby* (with CD)

### Language Arts Activity

Students will discuss, imitate, illustrate, and create ocean life in various ways: through visual art, spoken and written language

### Musical Activity

Students will sing, listen, play instruments and move

### Materials

"Aquarium" and "Personages with Long Ears," from *Carnival of the Animals*, by Camille Saint-Saëns

Scarves

Chart or board with sea sounds rhyme (see below)

Ocean drum, or some sort of sound effects for the ocean

Finger cymbals

Various pitched and nonpitched instruments

Painting supplies: water colors, black markers, mural-sized butcher paper

1. FOCUS. Play *Chorus of Whales* as students get settled. (Note: This is a recording of the sound of whales in their natural setting. If you have difficulty finding this particular recording, many such recordings and Web sites are easily accessible. Search the category "Whale Sounds.") Discuss ocean life. What creatures live in the ocean?

2. BODY OF LESSON. Invite children to read the following rhyme from a chart

    **Sea Sounds**
    I walked on the beach
    And picked up a shell
    And held it close to my ear.
    I walked on the beach
    And picked up a shell
    And held it close to my ear.
    And what did I hear?
    R-O-A-R S-w-i-s-h

R-O-A-R S-w-i-s-h

The sound of the sea I did hear.

3. Play an ocean drum or an upturned hand drum with a rubber ball or popcorn kernels. Allow students to play the ocean sound while teacher reads the rhyme. Invite students to create gestures with the poem—perform with the chant.

4. Listen to Saint-Saëns's "Aquarium." Students copy while teacher moves hands in fish-like motion. Students use movement to express the music, use scarves as fish.

5. Read *The Rainbow Fish* using the recording of "Aquarium" from *Carnival of the Animals* as a sound carpet. Experiment with tempo of reading—you might want to switch to "Personages with Long Ears" when you come to the section introducing the octopus.

6. Discuss the story. Why did Rainbow Fish feel happy at the end?

7. Discuss the mood of "Aquarium." Ask questions to help guide the discussion. Example: Is it bumpy and fast, or smooth and gentle, and so on?

8. Distribute finger cymbals, one per child. Play "Aquarium" again and encourage the children to move through the room as if through water, gently tapping their finger cymbal against a friend's.

9. LESSON EXTENSION. Read *The Whale's Song* while playing the recording of *Chorus of Whales* when the whales come into the story.


**More Books on the Ocean** (Compiled by Wilma Flanagan)

*Those Summers,* by Aliki. HarperCollins, 1996. A little girl remembers summers at the seashore where children swim, romp on the beach, collect shells, build sandcastles and enjoy other fun-filled activities.

*Secret Seahorse,* by Stella Blackstone; illustrated by Clare Beaton. Barefoot Books, 2004. A seahorse leads the reader past coral reefs and underwater creatures to a seahorse family hidden in a cave.

*D.W. All Wet,* by Marc Brown. Little, Brown, 1988. D.W. bosses her brother Arthur into carrying her on his shoulders at the beach because she maintains that she hates the water, until she gets a big wet surprise.

*Flip-Flops,* by Nancy Cote. Albert Whitman, 1998. Even though Penny is annoyed that she can only find one of her flip-flops on the day she goes to the beach, she discovers a number of uses for it and enjoys her time there.

*The Boy on the Beach,* by Niki Daly. Margaret K. McElderry Books, 1999. Reluctant to let the surf crash over him, Joe runs down the beach and has an adventure with an old boat.

*The Sand Children,* by Joyce Dunbar; illustrated by Mark Edwards. Crocodile Books, 1999. A boy and his father make a sand giant while camping at the beach, and during the night it comes to life to make sand children.

*Six Sandy Sheep,* by Judith Ross Enderle and Stephanie Gordon Tessler; illustrated by John O'Brien. Boyds Mills Press, 1997. Six sheep can't seem to stay out of trouble when they go to the beach.

*The Old Ball and the Sea,* by Warren Gebert. Bradbury Press, 1988. A boy and his dog spend the day at the beach building sand castles, watching ships and playing with the ball that washes ashore.

*Beach Play,* by Marsha Hayles; illustrated by Hideko Takahashi. Henry Holt, 1998. The sunny beach offers many fun and exciting activities for those who spend a day playing on its warm sands and in the water.

*Spot Goes to the Beach,* by Eric Hill. Putnam, 1985. His parents take Spot the puppy to the beach for a fun-filled day. Flaps conceal parts of the illustrations.

*Sally Goes to the Beach,* by Stephen Huneck. Abrams, 2000. Sally, a black Labrador retriever, goes to the beach, where she enjoys various activities with other visiting dogs.

*Grandma Summer,* by Harley Jessup. Viking, 1999. On a visit with Grandma to the old family summer house at the shore, Ben finds both the beach and the house filled with history and treasures waiting to be discovered.

*Down at the Bottom of the Deep Dark Sea,* by Rebecca C. Jones; illustrated by Virginia Wright-Frierson. Bradbury Press, 1991. Andrew hates water and intends to stay away from the ocean while at the beach, but he changes his mind when he needs water for the sand city he is building.

*Grandma and the Pirate,* by David Lloyd; illustrated by Gill Tomblin. Crown Publishers, 1986. At the beach a little boy pretends to be a pirate until his grandmother neatly turns the tables.

*How Will We Get to the Beach?* by Brigitte Luciani; illustrated by Eve Tharlet. North-South Books, 2000. The reader is asked to guess what Roxanne must leave behind (ball, umbrella, book, turtle or baby) as she tries various means of transportation to get to the beach.

*Rhinos Who Surf,* by Julie Mammano. Chronicle Books, 1996. Rhinos who surf get up early, paddle out and have fun until the sun goes down, when they ride the last wave to shore. Includes surfer lingo and a glossary of terms.

*The Happy Hippopotami,* by Bill Martin Jr.; illustrated by Betsy Everitt. Harcourt Brace Jovanovich, 1970. The happy hippopotami enjoy a merry holiday at the beach, wearing pretty beach pajamas, dancing the maypole or battling with water guns.

*Lottie's New Beach Towel,* by Petra Mathers. Atheneum Books for Young Readers, 1998. Lottie the chicken has a number of adventures at the beach, during which her new towel comes in handy.

*Tom and Pippo on the Beach,* by Helen Oxenbury. Candlewick Press, 1993. Tom and his stuffed monkey Pippo trade sun hats when they go to the beach with Daddy.

*Beach Days,* by Ken Robbins. Viking Kestrel, 1987. Hand-tinted photographs and simple, poetic text re-create the fun of a beach trip.

*At the Beach,* by Anne and Harlow Rockwell. Macmillan, 1987. A child experiences enjoyable sights and sounds during a day at the beach.

*Ebb and Flo and the Greedy Gulls,* by Jane Simmons. Margaret K. McElderry Books, 1999. Somebody has stolen the picnic sandwiches, and Ebb runs away when she is accused of being the thief.

*One Seal,* by John Stadler. Orchard Books, 1999. A boy runs after his kite down to the beach and meets an amazing assortment of animals who help him get his kite back—temporarily.

*Sand Castle,* by Brenda Shannon Yee; pictures by Thea Kliros. Greenwillow Books, 1999. Jen starts to build a sand castle at the beach, and others come along to help make the moat, path, wall and road around it.

### Lesson 4 by Regina Carlow: Pizza Pizza Daddy-O

This lesson combines the excitement of a favorite food, a rousing call-and-response singing game and a creative writing activity.

*Book/Literature*

*Pizza at Sally's,* by Monica Wellington
*A Pizza the Size of the Sun,* by Jack Prelutsky

*Language Arts Activity*

Create an original recipe for pizza

*Musical Activity*

Play a call-and-response singing game
Improvise to a chant with steady beat
Keep beat with rhythm instruments

*Materials*

Rhythm instruments
Jump rope
Construction paper

1. FOCUS. Teacher does this chant in a line by line echo style with children.

*The Pizza Chant*

Big

Big and Hot

Big, Hot and Juicy

Eatalota, Eatalota, Eatalota Pizza

Oh no more Italian pizza

Pepperoni, mushrooms, anchovies on the pizza

Mozzarella cheese, and Parmesan too

Doesn't matter kind of pizza, doesn't matter no!

It's Mmmm, Mmmm good!

2. Teacher asks students what toppings they like on pizza. Lists them on a chart or on chalk board. Teacher tells students to remember their favorite topping.

3. Children chant their favorite toppings around a circle. Try to get all the way around the circle keeping the beat with no misses. (Repeated toppings are okay!)

4. Teacher reads *Sally's Pizza.*

5. Students write original recipes for their own pizzas.

6. Play *Pizza Pizza Daddy-O*—chant or sing (see Appendix B).

| **Solo (call)** | **Group (response)** |
|---|---|
| Jenny's got a boyfriend | Pizza Pizza Daddy O! |
| How'd' you know it? | Pizza Pizza Daddy O! |
| Cause she told me | Pizza Pizza Daddy-O! |
| Let's dance it! | Pizza Pizza Daddy-O! |
| Let's twist it! | Pizza Pizza Daddy-O! |
| Let's hop it! | Pizza Pizza Daddy-O! |

a. Children get into a circle with someone going inside the middle.

b. The children on the outside chant, "So-n-so's [Jenny's] got a boy/girlfriend! Pizza, Pizza Daddy-O!"

c. The person in the middle responds, "How'd you know it?"

d. Children in the circle chant back "Pizza, Pizza Daddy-O!"

e. Then the person in the middle says, "Cause she told me!"

f. Circle children respond "Pizza, Pizza Daddy-O!"

g. Person in the middle now gives commands for motions for the whole group saying "Let's . . . " (fill in that blank) and begins to mime that action while the others in the circle mimic that person, saying "Pizza, Pizza Daddy-O!" For example, if the person in the middle said, "Like a rock star," then everyone would mimic a rock star.

h. The person in the middle takes three or four turns "like a . . . " depending on what they want to do.

i. Finally, when he/she has had enough of being in the middle, he/she says, "like so-n-so" (who is in the circle). That person then comes into the circle and the game starts again.

7. LESSON EXTENSION

A. Read the story *A Pizza the Size of the Sun* by Jack Prelutsky. This wonderful poem can be sung to the tune of "On Top of Old Smokey" or chanted with rhythm accompaniment.

B. Invite children to create their own pizza poems or vocal raps.

C. Share the book *Pizza Counting* by Christine Dobson. Encourage children to create their own Pizza Numbers Art.


**More Books on Pizza** (Compiled by Wilma Flanagan)

*Pizza Pat,* by Rita Golden Gelman; illustrated by Will Terry. Random House, 1999. A cumulative rhyme describes the choppy cheese, sloppy sausages, gloppy tomatoes and floppy dough that are cooked into a pizza and enjoyed by dozens of mice.

*Little Nino's Pizzeria,* by Karen Barbour. Harcourt Brace Jovanovich, 1987. Tony likes to help his father at their small family restaurant, but everything changes when Little Nino's Pizzeria becomes a fancier place.

*A Job for Wittilda*, by Caralyn and Mark Buehner. Dial Books for Young Readers, 1993. When Wittilda the witch is forced to look for a job, she finds her broom-flying ability comes in handy in applying for a job delivering pizzas.

*Curious George and the Pizza,* edited by Margret Rey and Alan J. Shalleck. Houghton Mifflin, 1985. Curious George creates havoc in a pizza shop but redeems himself by making an unusual delivery.

*How Pizza Came to Queens,* by Dayal Kaur Khalsa. C.N. Potter, 1989. An Italian visitor to Queens bemoans the unavailability of pizza until some thoughtful girls enable her to make some.

*Pizza for Breakfast,* by Maryann Kovalski. Morrow Junior Books, 1991. Frank and Zelda learn the folly of making wishes when they ask for more customers at their pizza restaurant.

*Pizza Party,* by Grace Maccarone; illustrated by Emily Arnold McCully. Cartwheel Books, 1994. A group of children have fun making a pizza.

*Pete's a Pizza,* by William Steig. HarperCollins, 1998. When Pete feels miserable because rain makes it impossible to play ball outdoors, his father finds a fun indoor game to play with his son.

*"Hi, Pizza Man!"* by Virginia Walter; pictures by Ponder Goembel. Orchard Books, 1995. While a young girl waits for the delivery of a hot pizza, she provides the appropriate animal sounds for a variety of pretend animal pizza deliverers.

*Huggly's Pizza,* by Tedd Arnold. Scholastic, 2000. Huggly and his monster friends, Booter and Grubble, set out to find the yummy human food he has tried, pizza.

*The Little Red Hen Makes a Pizza,* retold by Philemon Sturges; illustrated by Amy Walrod. Dutton Children's Books, 1999. In this version of the traditional tale, the duck, the dog and the cat refuse to help the Little Red Hen make a pizza but do get to participate when the time comes to eat it.

## Lesson 5 by Julia Church Hoffman: Fresh Fall Leaves

This lesson features a **sound carpet (accompaniment)** to create a mood in story about a beautiful day in the fall.

### *Grade*

Kindergarten or 1st Grade

### *Book/Literature Selection*

*Fresh Fall Leaves*, by Betsy Franco and Shari Halpern

*Leaf Man,* by Lois Ehlert

### *Early Literacy Goals*

Print motivation and narrative skills

### *Musical Goals*

Using different voices

Performing movement with a partner

Performing improvised movement

Playing instruments to illustrate text of poem

### *Materials/Resources Needed*

A recording of Saint-Saëns's *Carnival of the Animals*, "Aquarium" as a sound carpet

Multicolored silk scarves (one for each child)

Pitched/nonpitched percussion instruments

1. FOCUS. Teacher and student discuss various activities associated with autumn leaves (rake them, throw them, pile them, etc.).

2. Teacher sings or chants "Leaves Are Twirling" (sing to tune "Are You Sleeping?"). Children move like falling leaves.

> Leaves are twirling
> Leaves are twirling
> all around
> all around
> They are falling softly
> Very, Very softly
> to the ground.

3. Teacher recites "Autumn Leaves" (motions in brackets).

> Autumn leaves are all around [encircle imaginary leaves with your arms or with a partner arms around]
> falling falling to the ground [hands imitate falling leaves while voice falls, make leaves fall down partner's back]
> rake them up in one big pile ["rake" leaves, rake partner's back]
> Now . . . jump right in [*jump* in the pile, jump to do motions to your partner]
> with a great big smile [smile].

4. Read and discuss *Fresh Fall Leaves*. Add instruments to complement the text—children can determine for example:

   - a "crunchy" sounding instrument—e.g., shaker
   - something that "falls," e.g., move down a glockenspiel
   - a "rake"—e.g., a guiro
   - Jump—e.g., a drum
   - Smile—e.g., a finger cymbal

5. Recite the poem modeling how to play the instruments; then do just the instruments and ask children to move to the sound of the instruments.

6. If you have illustrations of each line of the poem, you could have the children sequence the visuals—what is first, next, and so on?

7. LESSON EXTENSION. Do the same lesson with *Leaf Man* by Lois Ehlert.

### Lesson 6 by Kay Martin: Pumpkin Pumpkin!

This lesson involves the use of gestures and motions to a song about the life cycle of a plant. Children are invited to create an original poem or story.

*Grades*

Kindergarten or 1st Grade

*Book/Literature Selection*

*Pumpkin Pumpkin,* by Jeanne Titherington

*Language Arts Activity*

Describe the plant cycle process

Draw a veggie-growing scenario of student's choice

*Musical Activity*

Chanting and improvisation on a steady beat

Dramatization of a song with movement

*Materials*

Pumpkin chant

Visuals of various types of vegetables

Paper and crayons

1. FOCUS. Chant this rhyme while patting a steady beat.

> Pumpkin Pumpkin
> Round and fat
> You can make a jack-o-lantern
> Just like that!

2. Teacher encourages children to walk a steady beat and invites children to take turns suggesting jack-o-lantern facial expressions—and in the space after the phrase "Just like that!" all will create a jack-o-lantern (Halloweenesque) face.

3. Read the book to the students.

4. Ask questions about what happened first, second, and so on.

5. Ask questions about contents in the pictures, for example, "What animal do you see? Who else is in the garden? Whose feet?"

6. Ask, "How can we move to the words?" Example: "How do you move when you plant? How can we show a plant growing?"

7. Sing the following song and do motions.

*The Farmer and His Seeds* (To the tune of "The Farmer in the Dell")

> The farmer plants the seeds, [Stoop and pretend to plant seeds]
> The farmer plants the seeds
> Hi, Ho, the dairy-o,
> The farmer plants the seeds.

Additional verses:

| | |
|---|---|
| The sun comes out to shine | [Make a large circle with arms] |
| The rain begins to fall | [Hands flutter up and down] |
| The seeds begin to grow | [Stand up slowly] |
| The farmer cuts them down | [Cutting motion] |
| He binds them into sheaves | [Stand close together] |
| And now we'll have some bread. | [Pretend to eat] |

8. Teacher initiates discussion about the plant life cycle. Shows visuals of various vegetables and distributes paper and crayons and invites children to create their own life cycle drawing.

9. LESSON EXTENSION. Children can take their drawings of plant cycle and create a poem or a story based on their artwork.

**Lesson 7 by Kay Martin: Three Little Bears!**

This lesson combines the creation of original poetry and a rhythm sound piece from key vocabulary words in the story.

### *Grade*

Late 1st or 2nd Grade

### *Book/Literature Selection*

*The Berenstain Bears and the Spooky Old Tree,* by Stan and Jan Berenstain

### *Language Arts Activity*

Children will create a class poem from repetitive words in the story

### *Musical Activity*

Perform a rhythm sound piece

*Materials:*

A card or poster that says CLAP THE RHYTHM on one side and SAY THE WORDS on the other

Triangles, claves, drums, rhythm sticks, ratchets

Chart paper

1. FOCUS. Have the words "Three Little Bears" on a chart and invite the children to chant the rhythm of the words. Next have them clap the rhythm of the words without speaking.

2. The teacher verbally challenges the children to either CLAP THE RHYTHM or SAY THE WORDS while keeping a steady beat at a visual prompt as the teacher now silently flips card (as mentioned above).

3. The teacher introduces the story and then reads the story, speaking loudly on the lines, "Yes, they dare."

4. Teacher asks the students to identify the phrases that were repeated. Isolate "Yes, they dare." Teacher invites children to join in on that phrase in the next reading.

5. Teacher isolates the text (show text on a chart):

   > One with a light.
   > One with a rope.
   > One with a stick.

6. Teacher instructs children to clap after each sentence.

7. Next uses the following rhythm instruments to punctuate the text: With the triangle, play after the word "light." With the claves, play after the word "stick." With the drum, play after the word "rope." With the ratchet, play after the word "shivers." With the rhythm sticks, tap out the rhythm of the words "three little bears" after the words are spoken.

8. Teacher takes the words stick, rope, shivers, light and presents an original poem (this should already be written).

9. Teacher invites children to create a short class poem using the same text.

10. LESSON EXTENSION. Students will perform class poem as a rhythm sound piece. Students will create individual poems from key words in the story.

## Lesson 8 by Jan Delgado: Descriptive Words

This lesson explores the artistic use of onomatopoeia in music and children's literature.

## Grade

1st or 2nd Grade

## Books/Literature Selections

*Mortimer,* by Robert Munsch

*The Listening Walk*, by Paula Showers

## Language Arts Activity

Generate lists of onomatopoetic words

## Musical Activity

Use vocal inflection, body percussion and pitch exploration to add drama to a story

## Materials

Chart or board listing the following descriptive words: Buzz, zoom, bang, fizz, pop, crackle, snap, crunch, tick tock, sizzle, boom, smack, clap, honk, ping, twinkle, thud, splash, whoosh, cuckoo, meow, bark, moo, neigh, tweet, cricket

Rhythm instruments

1. FOCUS. Children say the following chant patting a steady beat:

    > Clang, clang, rattle-bing-bang
    > Gonna make my noise all day
    > Clang, clang, rattle-bing-bang
    > Gonna make my noise all day.

2. Teacher invites children to make up rhythm clapping pattern that enhances "Rattle-bing-bang."

3. Play rhythm instruments with chant.

4. BODY OF LESSON. Using the words "thump thump thump thump thump" starting with low vocal inflection move to high inflection. Reverse the order of high to low.

5. Teacher reads *Mortimer* once through.

6. On the second reading teacher challenges children to create character voices to perform the "Thump thump" sections.

7. Teacher reads descriptive words on white board or chart: Buzz, zoom, bang, fizz, pop, crackle, snap, crunch, tick tock, sizzle, boom, smack, clap, honk, ping, twinkle, thud, splash, whoosh, cuckoo, meow, bark, moo, neigh, tweet, cricket.

8. Teacher encourages children to select rhythm instruments that match the onomatopoetic words.

9. LESSON EXTENSION. Do the same lesson using *Goin' on a Bear Hunt* by Michael Rosen and *The Listening Walk* by Paula Showers.

### Lesson 9 by Carla Haynes: Wishy Washy!

An extension of Lesson 8, this lesson uses the sounds of a washing machine as a starting point for musical and poetic improvisation.

### *Grade*

Kindergarten or 1st Grade

### *Book/Literature Selection*

*Mrs. Wishy Washy*, by Joy Cowley

### *Language Arts Activity*

Create a short chant based on mud sounds

Create a poem based on washing machine sounds

### *Musical Objective*

Create a spoken **rhythmic ostinato** based on the mud poem below

Create a rhythm sound piece based on washing machine sounds

Experiment with musical form

1. FOCUS. Teacher reads the following poem to children.

> Mud is very nice to feel
> All squishy-squashy between the toes.
> I'd rather wade in wiggly mud,
> Then smell a yellow rose.
> Nobody else but the rosebud knows
> How nice mud feels
> Between the toes.

2. Teacher challenges children to create a short phrase based on mud sounds to accompany the poem (e.g., *Squishy Squishy Plop*) for a second reading.

3. BODY OF LESSON. Students gather and teacher reads *Mrs. Wishy Washy*. On second reading teacher invites students to join in on the phrase, "Oh, lovely mud." Experiment with adding other layers of text (perhaps the mud chant from the poem above).

4. Before reading again, assign motions/gestures to the following selected words.

| | |
|---|---|
| "Plop" | Hands up and down at the same time |
| "Roll" | Hands side to side, same direction, same time |
| "Pit-pat" | Same as "Plop," but alternating. |
| "Wishy-washy" | Same as "Roll," except in opposite directions |
| "Go-Aways" | "Plop," "Roll," "Pit-pat," big bars to small |
| "Splat" | One sound, both hands down at the same time |

5. Teacher reads book again and students perform movements to assigned words.

6. Teacher leads discussion to subject of washing clothes after playing in the mud. Challenges students to create words that sound like a washing machine.

7. Teacher helps children create a poem

8. LESSON EXTENSION. Students and teachers choose appropriate instrument accompaniment.

9. *Read Mrs. Wishy Washy* combining created poem, mud ostinato and instrumental accompaniment to experiment with musical form.

### Lesson 10 by Julia Church Hoffman: Monsters and Dinosaurs

This lesson uses the song "Dem Bones" as a way of connecting two intriguing themes: dinosaurs and monsters. Teacher and students are challenged to respond to various musical prompts.

### *Grade*

Kindergarten

### *Book/Literature Selection*

*Happy Birthday, Frankie,* by Sarah Weeks; illustrated by Warren Linn

*Dem Bones*, by Bob Barner

*Dinosaur Bones,* by Bob Barner

### *Literacy Activity*

Writing stories, drawing pictures—sharing with others about what would happen if they were put together differently

Science—bones, body parts

*Musical Activity*

Singing

Listening, responding and moving to a recorded selection

*Materials/Resources Needed*

"Fossils" from Saint-Saëns's *Carnival of the Animals*

1. Play recording of "Fossils," from Saint-Saëns's *Carnival of the Animals*. Teacher challenges students to listen for the xylophone part. Teacher instructs, "When you hear it do something (like touch your nose, shake your hands, etc.) when you don't hear the sound sit still" (or other contrasting activity).

2. Talk about fossils, bones, how we're put together, and so on.

3. Sing (or chant) "Dem Bones" with the book of the same name.

4. Compare *Dem Bones* with *Dinosaur Bones*.

5. Play *Fossils* recording and invite children to dance like a skeleton during the xylophone, freeze in the other parts.

6. LESSON EXTENSION. Read *Happy Birthday, Frankie*. Teacher initiates discussion about how we would look if we were put together differently. Draw or paint pictures of what you would look like.

7. Transcribe children's descriptions of their drawings into stories or original songs (could use the "Dem Bones" melody/rhythm).

8. Share drawings and explanations with classmates.

## REFERENCES

Barner, Bob. *Dem Bones*. New York: Chronicle Books, 1996.

Barner, Bob. *Dinosaur Bones*. New York: Chronicle Books, 2001.

Berenstain, Stan and Jan. *The Berenstain Bears and the Spooky Old Tree*. New York: Random House for Young Readers, 1978.

Birdseye, Tom, Debbie Holdsclaw, and Andrew Glass. *She'll Be Comin' Round the Mountain*. New York: Holiday House, 1994.

Blake, Quentin. *Clown*. New York: Henry Holt, 1998.

Canyon, Christopher, and John Denver. *John Denver's Ancient Rhymes: A Dolphin Lullaby* (with CD). Nevada, CA: Dawn Publications, 2004.

Carle, Eric. *From Head to Toe*. New York: Harper Trophy, 1999.

Correa-Connolly, Melissa. *Ninety-Nine Activities and Greetings: Great for Morning Meetings . . . And Other Meetings Too!* Turners Falls, MA: Northeast Foundation for Children, 2004.

Cowley, Joy. *Mrs. Wishy Washy*. New York: Philomel, 1999.

Dillon, Leo and Dianne. *Rap a Tap Tap: Here's Bojangles—Think of That!* New York: Scholastic, The Blue Sky Press, 2002.

Ehlert, Lois. *Fresh Fall Leaves*. New York: Harcourt Children's Book, 2005.

Franco, Betsey, and Shari Halpern. *Fresh Fall Leaves*. New York: Scholastic, 1994.

Grogan, John, and Richard Cowdrey. *Bad Dog, Marley!* New York: Harper Collins, 2007.

Heiligman, Deborah, and Tim Bowers. *Fun Dog, Sun Dog*. New York: Scholastic, 2005.

Jackson, Alison, and Tricia Tusa. *Ballad of Valentine*. New York: Dutton Juvenile, 2002.

Moomaw, Sally. *Discovering Music in Early Childhood*. Boston: Allyn and Bacon, 1984.

Trapini, Iza. *The Itsy Bitsy Spider*. Watertown, MA: Charlesbridge, 1993.

Turner, Barrie C., and Sue Williams. *Carnival of the Animals: Classical Music for Kids*. New York: Henry Holt, 1999.

Wellington, Monica. *Pizza at Sally's*. New York: Dutton Juvenile, 2006.

Wirth, Marian, Verna Stassevitch, Rita Shotwell, and Patricia Stemmler. *Musical Games, Fingerplays and Rhythmic Activities for Early Childhood*. West Nyack, NY: Parker, 1983.

# CHAPTER 6

# *Working with the Intermediate Grades: 3–5*

Although children in the intermediate grades show growth and development that follow reasonably predictable patterns, growth is deeply influenced by culture, personality and environment. Many academic, social and physical "spurts" happen between the period in which a child moves between grades three, four, and five. Eight-year-olds may be physically awkward trying out a new game involving ball bouncing or hand clapping and by the time they are in the fifth grade, those skills have not only become very easy, they can also be filled with social innuendo that were not present before.

Third graders often prefer games and activities that release great amounts of energy and generally favor pairing with the same gender. In large groups they often band together to form a strong core and display an "all for one" front on an important task or challenge. In the area of creating or improvising, small group work is almost always the most efficient means of getting the job done. Likewise, peer criticism and acceptance is quite important. A sense of fairness and moral responsibility is beginning to develop. With this in mind, third graders are beginning to understand the multiple layers of storyline, social concerns and moral issues present in ballads, epic poems and longer folk tales. The length of these works should be kept on a smaller scale, with the concentration on the academic content and issues at hand.

Children in the fourth grade are often more physically coordinated and push themselves hard, sometimes to exhaustion, on a physical task. This is a time when competitiveness is at its peak, so "boys against girls" games are popular as are individual winners provided these games are presented with lightheartedness, fun and nonsarcastic humor. Fourth graders are usually highly sensitive to criticism from adults as well as peers. With proper preparation, children at this age can feel confident performing or improvising on an instrument or suggesting a physical activity or movement. Because of a love of and facility with language and vocabulary, fourth graders are often quite adept at writing original poems or setting new lyrics to well-known songs.

By the time they enter the fifth grade, children have become the most actively receptive (Wood, 1997) as learners of factual information. This, then, is an excellent time to present longer poems and songs with multiple verses. Fifth graders can and will memorize the text and will happily recite them back to you upon request. Because fifth graders generally are a cooperative group, full group work is often a joy. Fairness and empathy can be practiced and reinforced through teacher modeling and requests. Choral reading or class plays hinging on a moral theme are very popular activities that work well with the naturally ebullient fifth grader.

### But What about Dolores?

The fifth-grade chorus was seated on the risers facing their teacher, Miss Sampson, as she read them a story. This normally rambunctious group was sitting quietly and seemed to be listening carefully even though they as a whole considered themselves "too old" to be read to by the teacher. The teacher read:

> "I'm sorry, Dolores," Moustro Provolone said. He had a sad look on his face as if he had just eaten blue cheese. "You're very enthusiastic, but I'm afraid your singing is just a little too . . . loud."
> "I can sing softly," Dolores said.
> Moustro Provolone began to squirm as if he had just eaten *bad* blue cheese. "It isn't only that Dolores. I'm afraid you just don't have an ear for music."
> "Of course I do!" Dolores shouted. "I have two of them." Dolores stomped off in a huff. (—From "Horace and Morris Join the Chorus: But What about Dolores?" by James Howe)

The students listened as their teacher continued reading the story about the determined Dolores, who, despite her music teacher's opinion of her singing abilities, pursued membership in the school chorus. Eddie, a sandy-haired boy with a fine mass of light tan freckles was sitting on the end of the second row. He had been having trouble with his voice lately. He was in the beginnings of his voice change and his voice was sometimes several octaves higher and sometimes completely monotone and could be heard above the chorus as they sang. Several of the children made faces when he sang and some refused to stand next to him.

As Miss Sampson read the story, a few children nervously glanced in Eddie's direction. When she finished the story, she instructed the chorus to stand and sing "Hold Fast to Dreams," a choral piece set to the text of a poem by Langston Hughes. As the group sang, Eddie in his nervousness, stopped singing altogether. But Roy, the boy standing next to him, whispered in his ear, "Man, you have the best low notes in the whole chorus." Eddie smiled and then began to sing out.

## SINGING IN THE INTERMEDIATE GRADES

Unless children have had positive experiences singing as younger children, they will often show great reluctance to sing in the intermediate grades. There are a number of reasons for this. Certainly, the societal stigma of singing is one. But also, at this age, boys' voices are beginning to change (some as young as nine years old); if boys have not had positive singing experiences before their voices change, they are often reluctant to sing if there is the slightest chance they could stick out vocally.

If you find that the children you are working with are not used to singing as a group, then chanting and choral readings are an excellent way to combine their interest in story line, new vocabulary and spoken art forms. It is also important to let children hear appropriate vocal models such as children's choruses and solo singers and to call attention to the differences between singing and speaking.

Discussion of the voice change is also appropriate. Simply put, I let students know that all voices grow and change. With boys it is more dramatic and we can hear it much more clearly than with girls. One of the reasons behind this is that boys have a longer way to go to make the change from the high voice of a child to the low voice of a man. Usually this simple explanation is enough to help the class understand the basics of the process.

If the children I am working with have had positive experiences with singing, then I find that **ballads** and story songs are a great challenge enjoyed by all. I find that **verse, refrain** songs, that connect directly to content in social studies and language arts classes are quite popular. One activity that children enjoy is to take lyrics from a popular tune (teacher-approved, of course!) that connects to a story or area to be studied and distribute the words and invite children to sing it starting at their own comfortable range as a class. Students love to share what they consider to be "their music" with their teachers.

Interdisciplinary themes are also important. When I was an elementary music teacher, classroom teachers and librarians would frequently request songs based on themes they might be covering in class. I took this one step further, organizing entire concerts and learning units on a single theme per grade level. I found that the intermediate elementary students enjoyed making the many connections with the songs we sang in music class to content they were studying.

## PLAYING INSTRUMENTS

Because physical coordination is steadily increasing throughout elementary school, many students in the intermediate grades have already begun private musical instruction on solo instruments. Some children are able to read **musical notation** and many are able to play by ear on their instruments. Rhythmically, students are able to create more intricate rhythmic patterns and in some cases are able to layer several musical lines, playing several different **rhythmic patterns** at the same time.

An easy way to do this is to think of these patterns as distinct lines in a poem. Allow students to experiment with playing the rhythm that sounds like the words. Each line has its own rhythm and sense of pulse. Some lines are repeated for effect. These phrases can become anchors for a choral speaking presentation. For example, the poem "The Blues" by Toyomi Igus, is a poem about the history of the art form the blues with possibilities for such an activity.

I would probably start by inviting the children to agree how they should say the lines in rhythm. Then I'd assign that rhythm to a small group, and I'd invite the entire class to chant all lines of the poem. Next, I'd show the entire poem and have them perform it the same way, then inviting students to create a rhythmic pattern for another line. After it is thoroughly practiced, I'd invite them to layer the pattern on top of the first pattern. I would continue challenging children to come up with different layers until the class as a group is satisfied with our composition.

I have also created many lessons with **polyrhythms,** which are several rhythms played at the same time. An excellent introduction to this is to listen to examples of West African drumming. Children love to layer hand drum patterns and enjoy experimenting with the many different sounds with found instruments.

## USING RECORDINGS

Children in the intermediate grades can listen for longer periods of time and are beginning to develop more abstract reasoning. Using recordings to enhance a book or character sometimes selecting music that sounds "heroic" or "adventurous" can be a wonderful hook for a story or a means to what they know about the character to a musical idea. I find that children at this age love to listen to music from other cultures and are eager to learn new facts about the culture. Many of the lessons following this chapter are built on folk tales and stories that highlight culture, issues of ethnic diversity and stereo-types and generalizations about various cultures. Most of the lessons that follow invite you to select your favorite recordings of mariachi music, Celtic music, vocal or instrumental jazz. Christine Strickland, Jan Delgado, Luis Delgado, Regina Stella Watkins, Sara Hutchinson and Donna Moore contributed lesson plans for the lesson ideas that follow.

## LESSON IDEAS FOR THE INTERMEDIATE GRADES

### Lesson 1 by Christine Strickland: Native American Dances

This lesson leads children and teacher to discuss cross-cultural traditions and to explore the relationship between movement and key vocabulary.

### *Grade*

3rd or 4th

## Book/Literature Selection

*Dancing with the Indians,* by Angela Shelf Medearis; illustrated by Samuel Byrd

*Rattlesnake Dance* by Jim Arnosky

## Language Arts Activity

Use vocabulary words—twist, writhe, coil and curl—to create an action story or poem

## Musical Activity

Maintain a steady beat with feet in time to a drum

Improvised movement from leader in response to vocabulary words

## Materials

Large drum

Several rattles or maracas

Chart or chalk board

1. FOCUS. Teacher has the following excerpt (poem) from the book and leads discussion of underscored words

   > Dancers join their hands
   > With every step they take,
   > They <u>twist</u> and <u>writhe</u> and <u>curl,</u>
   > The <u>coils</u> of a giant snake.

2. Teacher invites students to show movements of the words, and class selects the movements they like best and practice the movements as directed by teacher.

3. This can be done in four groups, inviting each group to present a movement based on one of the words.

4. BODY OF LESSON. Teacher previews the book by showing the cover illustration inviting students to predict what the story is about.

5. Teacher reads the story to students, checking for comprehension asking:

   - Who are the main characters in the story?
   - When does the story change from past to present; what are the clues?
   - What kinds of dances did the Indians in this story perform?
   - What purpose did the dances serve?
   - Why do you think Seminole Indians welcomed runaway slaves into their tribe?

6. Teacher refers back to the movements that were practiced earlier and selects a leader who will act as the "head of line" and one student who will perform a steady beat on the drum. Students are placed in a "snake line" holding hands and the "head of line" leads the class around the room improvising the movement words from the poem while the drummer is keeping a steady beat. Dancers' feet should match the beat of the steady drum.

7. Use the vocabulary words *twist, coil, writhe* and *curl* to create a poem or short story.

8. For a little extra challenge, gradually change the tempo of the beat to faster or slower. End the dance with a "snake line" coiled into a tight spiral.

9. LESSON EXTENSION. Read *Rattlesnake Dance.*

## Lesson 2 by Christine Strickland: The Ballad of Don Gato

This is a lesson/unit that combines a Spanish ballad and a traditional Mexican dance.

### Grades

4th or 5th

### Book/Literature Selection

*Señor Don Gato: A Traditional Song,* by Anonymous; illustrated by John Manders
*Celebrating Cinco de Mayo: Fiesta Time,* by Sandi Hill; illustrated by Claude Martinot

### Language Arts Activity

Explore lyrics to a ballad
Take lyrics and put them in a story map of events
Research variants of a folk song

### Musical Activity

Listen to a recording of mariachi music and a recording of the ballad of Don Gato
Students will learn about and dance the work dance "Los Machetes"

### Materials

Recording of "Señor Don Gato"
Recording of mariachi orchestra

Story map chart

Chart or chalkboard

1. FOCUS. Tell students they will be hearing a story based on a traditional ballad. Discuss key vocabulary: ballad, ardent, consultation, solar plexus, slated, reanimated.

2. Before reading story, teacher challenges students to remember the events in the story.

3. After reading the story, have the student tell the events as the remember them. Put them on a chart or a chalkboard.

4. Play recording of "Señor Don Gato" and ask students if the events are the same order in the song as in the book (some recordings will have different versions).

5. Give students a story map worksheet and then ask them to recount the events on the worksheet.

6. Have students dramatize story line, perhaps using one or more students as narrator.

7. LESSON EXTENSIONS. Locate Spain and Mexico on a map. Note the geographic distance and that there are two versions of the story of Don Gato: a Spanish and a Mexican version. Invite students to research the different story lines.

8. Read the book *Celebrating Cinco de Mayo: Fiesta Time.*

9. Teach students the dance: Los Machetes.

### Background Information for Los Machetes

The mariachi orchestra plays the music for the work dance Los Machetes. Mexican farm workers in the sugarcane fields created Los Machetes while they were cutting the cane. They spent a great deal of time perfecting the use of the tool (machete) for harvesting. Men usually wear a Mexican cowboy or *charro* outfit, which are black or brown suits with tight-fitting trousers trimmed down the sides with a double row of gold or silver buttons called *plata*. A white shirt and *rebozo*, a hanging, folded tie, is also worn. A large hat or *sombrero* completes the outfit.

*Formation:* Couples in two parallel lines (contra), facing each other. Below are three different parts or "actions" that can be used with most mariachi orchestra music. Depending on the music you select and the abilities of your students, you may do one, two or all three "actions" with a recording.

### Part A

1. March and clap facing front. Facing the music, march fourteen steps forward, clapping hands above head as you march. Turn to face the back on counts fifteen and sixteen.

2. March and clap facing back. Facing the back, march fourteen steps forward, clapping hands above head as you march. Turn to face partners with hands by sides on counts fifteen and sixteen.

## *Part B*

1. Facing partner, walk four steps backward away from partner. Walk forward back to place with four steps. Repeat.

2. Partner clap. Facing partner, clap both hands to partner's hands. Clap hands under own raised right knee. Put foot down and clap own hands in front of body. Clap hands under own raised left knee. Put foot down and clap own hands in front of body. Clap own hands behind back. Clap own hands in front three times quickly. You may do this section two times quickly (one clap per beat) or one time slowly (half-time or one clap per two beats).

## *Part C*

1. Star Formation. Partners raise right hands up high touching palm-to-palm, one dancer facing back, one facing the front. Walk forward with eight steps to return to place. Reverse: Raise left hands up high touching palm to palm, one dancer facing back, one facing the front. Walk forward with eight steps to return to place. Repeat.

2. Face front to start dance from beginning. Dance repeats three times and ends with marching pattern. End dance with a bow or curtsey during the three quick chords at the end.

### Lesson 3 by Christine Strickland: Rhythm Sticks

#### *Book/Literature Selection*

*Max Found Two Sticks,* by Brian Pinkney

*The Jazz Fly,* by Matthew Gollub

#### *Language Arts Activity*

Students will write lyrics to a scat tune and/or an original drum piece using onomatopoeia and present a glossary of their new scat/drum words

#### *Musical Activity*

Students will create and perform a rhythm composition

Students will improvise and sing their own scat tune

### *Materials*

Rhythm instruments

Some found instruments: trash cans, pots, paper cups, coffee cans, etc.

Recording of vocal jazz or blues (Ella Fitzgerald), see Appendix C

Chart or chalk board

1. FOCUS. Have the following text on a board. Invite the students to find a way to chant the words together.

> Pat-pat-tat. Putter-putter . . . pat-tat
> Tap-tat-tap. Tippy-tip . . . tat-tat
> Dum . . . dum-de-dum. Di-di-di-di. Dum-Dum.
> Dong . . . dang . . . dung. Ding . . . dong . . . ding!
> Cling . . . clang . . . da-BANG!
> A-cling-clang . . . DA-BANGGGGG!
> Thump-di-di-thump . . .
> THUMP-DI-DI-THUMP!

2. Show the students the cover of the book *Max Found Two Sticks* and ask them to predict the story line.

3. After discussion of what they think the book might be about, the teacher tells the students that the words they had just practiced will appear in the book. Teacher invites students to say the rhythms and to pat them on their laps or the floor during the reading. Teacher points to the text on the chart when it appears in the book.

4. After the story, discuss which patterns are meant to imitate the sounds in the book.

5. Next, teacher challenges students to use found instruments to play each line that might go along with the following words: *pigeons, rain, marching band, church bells* and *train*.

6. Teacher reads the story again with students supplying the instrumental accompaniment.

7. LESSON EXTENSION. Read *The Jazz Fly* by Matthew Gollub. Note that in *Max Found Two Sticks*, instruments were used to imitate sounds; in *The Jazz Fly*, vocal sounds are used to imitate instruments.

8. Encourage students to create scat words of their own and create a poem or a scat tune.

9. Students may also experiment with vocal percussion sounds from *Max Found Two Sticks* to create a drum riff using words.

### Lesson 4 by Donna Moore: Desert Sounds

### *Grade Level*

3rd–5th

*Book/Literature Selections*

*The Desert Is My Mother*, by Pat Mora

*Language Arts Activity*

Students will use expressive speech to communicate ideas.

*Music Objectives*

Students will read or perform, as a group, a poem, using vocal and instrumental sounds to enhance the poem

*Materials*

Assorted rhythm instruments, and/or found sounds

Chart paper or chalk board

1. FOCUS. Teacher leads session to brainstorm with students the word *desert* to access prior knowledge. Teacher leads them to think about desert animals, birds, reptiles, weather, sounds, and so on. Teacher asks them how they would feel in the desert and what they would hear and smell. Their responses are recorded on chart paper or a chalk board.

2. Read *The Desert Is My Mother* to the students. Discuss the setting and any events in the poem. Discuss the feeling or tone of the poem and any unfamiliar words.

3. Tell the students that we can reexperience this poem by reading or performing it in creative ways. Below are different ways to perform this poem. Use any or all.

- Assign solos, duets and small groups to read certain parts of the poem.
- Place students in different parts of the room, to get the effect of voices coming from all around. Practice.
- Lead students to use the range of their voices to give maximum expression.
- Have them practice projecting their voices so they can be heard.
- Practice enunciating clearly.
- Create a desert "sound environment" for the poem, using vocal sounds. This can be done at the beginning and end of the poem. Students should help in making these decisions. Discuss with them the kind of sounds that may be heard in the desert. They may need to do some research on weather, animals, birds and reptiles of certain deserts.
- Instruments can be used to help in the sound environment. Have a set of rhythm instruments handy for the students to choose from. Ideally, they will have had prior experience

with the instruments. If not, have a period of practice. Use a combination of vocal and instrument sounds.

- Choose some places within the poem where musical sound could be used, either as background or in pauses between lines or phrases.

4. LESSON EXTENSIONS. Ask the students what movements, if any, would enhance the reading of this poem. Try some of them out. Discuss and evaluate.

5. Explore other books and poetry about the desert. Consider *Listen to the Desert* (*Oye al Desierto*) by Pat Mora and Francisco Mora. This bilingual book illustrates the use of sound, rhythm and onomatopoeia. Also look at *Welcome to the Sea of Sand*, by Jane Yolen, and *This Big Sky*, by Pat Mora.

6. Lead the students to write their own poems about different environments. Lead them to create sound environments for their poems.

7. Create a work of art to illustrate any of these poems.

## Lesson 5 by Donna Moore: Desert Poetry

### Book/Literature Selection

*The Desert Is Theirs,* by Byrd Baylor; illustrated by Peter Parnall

*Desert Moods*, by Sara Hutchinson

### Language Arts Activity

Students will use illustrations and text prompts to develop original poems based on point of view

### Musical Activity

Students will imitate animals and ambient sounds in the desert through vocal and rhythmic improvisation

### Materials

Illustration of desert landscape (teacher could use student artwork from Lesson 4)

Chart or chalkboard

Point of view chart

Rhythm instruments

1. FOCUS. Teacher shows illustration of desert life and leads discussion of animals, plants and other life forms in the desert. Teacher leads to discussion of point of view.

2. BODY OF LESSON. Teacher reads story and asks students to think of the various points of view in the story.

3. Teacher presents the poem *Desert Moods,* inviting students to talk about the point of view from which it was written.

> *Desert Moods*
> The cactus wren
> Whose shady home's
> Tucked tight inside
> Saguaro's arm,
>
> Hunched and twitched
> A nervous quill,
> The inky clouds,
> A sudden chill,
>
> Foretold the torrent
> Slicing fast
> Through searing heat
> And dusty past.
>
> Zig zags of light,
> A thundering din,
> The cactus wren
> Retreats within.
>
> A whispering
> Of rising steam
> The desert is
> Renewed and clean.
>
> A satin pool
> In silence glints
> The slanting streaks of
> Fiery tints.
>
> Then tiny shards
> Like broken glass,
> The cactus wren
> Enjoys her bath.
> (By Sara Hutchinson, Dance Resource Teacher, Albuquerque Public Schools
> ARTS Center)

4. Students are invited to create an environment soundscape to accompany the poem. Sound environment possibilities:

- Vocal: "whoosh . . . shhhh" for wind and blowing sand, "sss" for rising steam, coyote sounds, eagle sounds, raindrop sounds.
- Instrumental: A rainstick may be used for rain or wind, maracas for snake sound, brushed drum for wind, and drum or trash can for thunder. A serrated woodblock (guiro woodblock) scraped rapidly five times sounds incredibly like a cactus wren!

5. Students may look up the cactus wren and listen to its call online at: birds.cornell.edu/AllAboutBirds/BirdGuideCactus_Wren/html#sound.

6. Teacher reviews characters from the story *The Desert Is Theirs*, and distributes point of view chart and asks students to choose a character from the story and complete the chart. This may be done as a class, individually or in small groups.

### Lesson 6 by Luis Delgado: Letter Puzzles

*Grades*

4th or 5th

*Book/Literature Selection*

*CDC?* by William Steig

*Language Arts Activity*

Students will have fun decoding and creating their own letter/number patterns

*Musical Activity*

Students will create rhythmic and melodic chants based on their own letter/number code patterns

*Materials*

Chart with code messages from the book *CDC*:

C U N 10-S-E

U F B-D I-S

E-R I M

D-2-R

Or . . . make up your own!

Rhythm instruments

Colored index cards (four or five colors for group work)

1. FOCUS. Teacher invites students to decode the secret messages on the chart.
2. BODY OF LESSON. Teacher reads *CDC* by William Steig.
3. Teacher helps students form into four or five groups and challenges students to compose an original short text message using numbers and letters.
4. Once the group has composed a message, they move to rhythm instruments to create rhythmic accompaniment for the message. Messages can also be sung.
5. After all groups have a musical message, they are performed for the entire group. LESSON EXTENSION. Take a text message and create an original poem or story. Show the poem *Txt U L8r* by Aislinn O'Loughlin (found in Cashman, Something Beginning with P: New Poems from Irish Poets)

## Lesson 7 by Regina Stella Watkins: A Musical Irish Day

### *Grades*

3rd or younger

### *Book/Literature Selection*

*Kathleen O'Byrne, Irish Dancer,* by Declan Carville and Brendan Ellis

### *Language Arts Activity*

Students will learn about proverbs, research proverbs and find one that rings true!

### *Musical Activity*

Dance an Irish jig

### *Materials*

Any jig recording

Collected Irish proverbs on chart:

   Life is like a cup of tea, it's all in how you make it!

   I complained that I had no shoes, Until I met a man who had no feet.

   There's no need to fear the wind if your haystacks are tied down.

If you lie down with dogs you'll rise with fleas.

An old broom knows the dirty corners best!

You've got to do your own growing, no matter how tall your grandfather was.

It's no use carrying an umbrella if your shoes are leaking.

1. FOCUS. Teacher shares Irish proverbs and asks students what they can learn from another culture by reading its proverbs.

2. Discuss what you might learn about Ireland from its proverbs.

3. BODY OF LESSON. Read book *Kathleen O'Byrne, Irish Dancer,* pointing out the girl's posture as she practices the Irish step dance everywhere: arms straight down.

4. At the end of the story, there is information about Irish dance. Invite children to take turns reading and sharing this information. (You may prefer to do this after children have learned a simplified Irish jig!)

5. Teach children the simplified step:

   - One count: hop on R foot, L leg cross in front
   - One count: hop on R foot, L leg cross behind
   - Two counts: L-R-L—step/step—step
   - Repeat with other leg. Keep alternating.

6. Read book again. Children should be able to identify the steps in the pictures. Ask them, "What does the story tell you about Irish culture?"

7. LESSON EXTENSION. Students will do research on proverbs and find one that rings true to them (their culture, family, etc.).

**Lesson 8 by Jan Delgado: Rooster's Off**

*Grades*

4th and 5th

*Book/Literature Selection*

*Rooster's Off to See the World,* by Eric Carle

*Language Arts Activity*

Using a range of voices, volumes, pacing and gestures perform book in a choral speaking style

## Musical Activity

Improvise and create melodic and rhythmic patterns for characters in the book to accompany choral speaking

## Materials

Assorted rhythm instruments

One or more xylophones

Wind chimes

Sentence strips with dialogue of characters in the book

*Rooster:* Come, see the world.
*Cats:* We would love to.
*Frogs:* Why not? We're not busy.
*Turtles:* Yes, it might be fun.
*Fish:* May we come along?

1. FOCUS. Preview book, make list of characters and order of appearance. Take note of the icons in the book that depict the order of performance. Put the words of the animals on sentence strips.

2. Read the book.

3. Practice saying the sentence strips in rhythm. Clap the rhythm of the words, then transfer to body percussion.

4. Divide the class into five groups, one of which is the rooster, another cats, and so on. Have each group practice their rhythm pattern by themselves. If need be, have only two parts at a time perform together so they can get used to staying on beat.

5. Practice layering the parts. Start with the rooster's pattern four times and continuing, then add the cats four times, then the frogs, turtle, the fish. Do it backward, with everyone starting at the same time, and then dropping out one at a time. Practice it loud and then softly.

6. Pick a narrator(s). They start reading the story and at every page with icons, the appropriate groups perform. At the part of the story where the animals start going home (dropping out), it is nice if the whole group just continues their parts but at a quieter dynamic so the narrators can be heard. Each part drops out as their animal leaves the story.

7. LESSON EXTENSION. Transfer body percussion to instruments. Make up melodies for the rhythms on xylophones or other pitched instruments.

8. Have groups of students make up their own patterns. Use percussion instruments to color some of the narration. For example, in the middle of the story at "The sun went down.

It began to get dark," use wind chimes and a xylophone tremolo. Have a sound for the moon as it appears several times.

### Lesson 9 by Regina Carlow: The Underground Railroad

*Grade*

3rd to 5th

*Book/Literature Selection*

*Follow the Drinking Gourd,* by Jeanette Winter
*Sweet Clara and the Freedom Quilt,* by Deborah Hopkinson

*Language Arts Activity*

Compose a journal entry or diary using codes from *Follow the Drinking Gourd.*

*Musical Activity*

Sing the song "Follow the Drinkin' Gourd" (see Appendix B)
Listen to a recording of "Harriet Tubman"

1. FOCUS. Play recording of "Harriet Tubman" and ask students to talk about the meanings of the following words: lifeline, first mate, pilgrim band.

2. Read the story and sing song if you wish "Follow the Drinkin' Gourd" (Appendix B) and challenge students to listen for code words.

3. Give background information for the Underground Railroad and some of the codes for the song "Follow the Drinkin' Gourd." Below is a verse-by-verse explanation of the codes.

"Follow the Drinkin' Gourd" is a coded song that gave slaves the route for an escape from Alabama and Mississippi. The route instructions were given to slaves by an old man named Peg Leg Joe. Working as an itinerant carpenter, he spent winters in the South, moving from plantation to plantation, teaching slaves this escape route.

> When the sun comes back and the first quail calls,
> Follow the Drinking Gourd.
> For the old man is waiting for to carry you to freedom,
> If you follow the Drinking Gourd.

"When the sun comes back" means winter and spring when the angle of the sun above the horizon at noon is getting higher each day. Quail are migratory birds which winter in the

South. The Drinking Gourd is the Big Dipper. The old man is Peg Leg Joe. The verse tells slaves to leave in the winter and walk toward the Drinking Gourd. Eventually they will meet a guide who will escort them for the remainder of the trip.

Most escapees had to cross the Ohio River which is too wide and too swift to swim. The Railroad struggled with the problem of how to get escapees across, and with experience, came to believe the best crossing time was winter. Then the river was frozen, and escapees could walk across on the ice. Since it took most escapees a year to travel from the South to the Ohio, the Railroad urged slaves to start their trip in winter in order to be at the Ohio River the next winter.

> The river bank makes a very good road,
> The dead trees show you the way,
> Left foot, peg foot, traveling on
> Follow the Drinking Gourd.

This verse taught slaves to follow the bank of the Tombigbee River north looking for dead trees that were marked with drawings of a left foot and a peg foot. The markings distinguished the Tombigbee from other north-south rivers that flow into it.

> The river ends between two hills,
> Follow the Drinking Gourd.
> There's another river on the other side,
> Follow the Drinking Gourd.

These words told the slaves that when they reached the headwaters of the Tombigbee, they were to continue north over the hills until they met another river. Then they were to travel north along the new river which is the Tennessee River. A number of the Southern escape routes converged on the Tennessee.

> Where the great big river meets the little river,
> Follow the Drinking Gourd.
> For the old man is awaiting to carry you to freedom if you
> Follow the Drinking Gourd.

This verse told the slaves the Tennessee joined another river. They were to cross that river (which is the Ohio River), and on the north bank, meet a guide from the Underground Railroad.

Teacher challenges students to write a journal entry with code words as if they were slaves escaping to freedom. Students may use the codes in the story or create original codes. Students who create new codes should provide a glossary of terms.

4. LESSON EXTENSION. Read *Sweet Clara and the Freedom Quilt* by Deborah Hopkinson.

5. Read: *My Name Is Georgia,* the story of Georgia O'Keeffe.

**Lesson 10 by Regina Carlow: Ballads**

*Grades*

4th and 5th

*Book/Literature Selection*

*Keep on Singing: A Ballad of Marian Anderson,* by Myra Cohn Livingston

*Language Arts Activity*

Analyze text to a ballad and compare the content with historical information

Fill out story board/sequence chart

*Musical Activity*

Learn about the life history of Marian Anderson through a narrative poem

Listen to a recording of Marian Anderson

Perform the ballad as a choral reading

*Materials*

Recording of Marian Anderson

Quote by Marian Anderson on chart or chalk board: "As long as you keep a person down, some part of you has to be down there to hold him down, so it means you cannot soar as you otherwise might."

Vocabulary words on flash cards: soprano, alto, tenor, bass, Jim Crow, ballad, Negro spiritual, Metropolitan Opera House, Constitution Hall, Lincoln Monument

1. FOCUS. Place the quote on chart or board and invite students to discuss what they think it means. You may use the Think-Pair-Share activity where students think on their own for a moment, then pair with another student in the class and then share their discussion with the entire class.

2. BODY OF LESSON. Teacher presents vocabulary words on flash cards to class and asks students to write down what they know about each term.

3. Teacher and students discuss their answers and then teacher reads the book *Keep on Singing.*

4. Teacher and students discuss the story noting that the italicized words in the story are Marian Anderson's actual words.

5. Teacher reads the Author's Notes to students.

6. Teacher plays recording of Marian Anderson.

7. Teacher and students look at the story and decide how it could be turned into a choral reading.

8. LESSON EXTENSION. Students prepare and perform the story for a performance.

9. Students could explore other ballads and stories that are also songs: Example: "The Ballad of John Henry" and "The Cat's in the Cradle."

10. Discuss the similarities and differences between the form of stories the *Ballad of Marian Anderson* and *My Name Is Georgia.*

## REFERENCES

Anonymous, and John Manders. *Señor Don Gato: A Traditional Song.* Cambridge, MA: Candlewick Press, 1993.

Arnosky, Jim. *Rattlesnake Dance.* New York: Penguin Putnam, 2000.

Baylor, Byrd, and Peter Parnall. *The Desert Is Theirs.* New York: Aladdin, 1987.

Carle, Eric. *Rooster's Off to See the World.* New York: Aladdin Picture Books, 1999.

Carville, Declan, and Brendan Ellis. *Kathleen O'Byrne, Irish Dancer.* Columbus, OH: Gingham Dog Press, 2003.

Cashman, Seamus. *Something Beginning with P: New Poems from Irish Poets.* Dublin: O'Brien Press, 2005.

Gollub, Matthew. *The Jazz Fly.* Santa Rosa, CA: Tortuga Press, 2000.

Hill, Sandi, and Claude Martinot. *Celebrating Cinco de Mayo: Fiesta Time.* Minneapolis, MN: Tandem Library Books, 2000.

Hopkinson, Deborah, and James Ransome. *Sweet Clara and the Freedom Quilt.* New York: Knopf, 1993.

Livingston, Myra Cohn. *Keep on Singing: A Ballad of Marian Anderson.* New York: Holiday House, 1994.

Medearis, Angela Shelf, and Samuel Byrd. *Dancing with the Indians.* New York: Holiday House, 1993.

Mora, Pat. *The Desert Is My Mother.* Houston, TX: Piñata Books, 1994.

Pinkney, Brian. *Max Found Two Sticks.* New York: Aladdin, 1997.

Steig, William. *CDC?* New York: Farrar, Straus and Giroux, 1986.

Winter, Jeanette. *My Name Is Georgia.* San Diego, CA: Voyager Books, 1998.

Winter, Jeanette, and Deborah Hopkinson. *Follow the Drinking Gourd.* Canada: Dragonfly Publishing, 1992.

Wood, Chip. *Yardsticks: Children in the Classroom Ages 4–14, A Resource for Parents and Teachers.* Turners Falls, MA: Northeast Foundation for Children, 1997.

# CHAPTER 7

## *Some Final Thoughts*

When we use musical ideas, concepts and activities to reinforce literacy skills, we are helping children develop invaluable connections with the content we want them to learn. Connecting books with music makes literature more meaningful and personal. When we present lessons that use music we increase our chances of reaching children who might not otherwise be engaged. Enhancing literature by listening to music, playing instruments, dancing and singing helps groups develop greater camaraderie, promotes creativity and sets up an environment of discovery in the classroom.

Musical experiences challenge children at differing levels and in some cases can ignite a child's quest for learning about something. Finding ways to include music in daily activities helps children become sustained, self-directed learners as they improvise, create, reflect and grow from extended explorations with a poem or book. In the following pages, I review strategies for integrating musical activities with children's literature, avenues to literacy and music connections and suggestions for using a recorded sound track or sound carpet with children's literature. Special thanks to Donna Moore, Jan Delgado and Julia Church Hoffman for their contributions to this chapter.

### SELECTING CHILDREN'S LITERATURE TO PAIR WITH MUSIC

When selecting children's literature to couple with music, movement or drama there are a number of characteristics to look for. First of all, repetition and pattern can be reinforced with chanting activities or can be used as a springboard for instrument playing or movement. For example, the pattern "Rap a Tap Tap—Think of That!" occurs fourteen times throughout the story *Rap a Tap Tap: Here's Mr. Bojangles—Think of That!* This short phrase pairs well with movement, drumming or exploration with vocal inflections. Eric Carle's *The Very Busy Spider* and Marjorie Dennis Murray's *Don't Wake Up the Bear* are books that present many opportunities for rhythmic speaking or chanting.

Look for opportunities to use **sound effects**. Invite children to examine a book to come up with words or phrases that will lend themselves to vocal percussion, found instruments or more traditional rhythm instruments. Children love to create a list of instruments that can be found at home that could be used to enhance a story. For example, children will enjoy creating sound effects for Gerald McDermott's *Papagayo the Mischief Maker.*

Sometimes **action words** can be used as a springboard to sound effects. You might want to ask children to create nonverbal sounds that describe running, leaping, floating, pouncing or falling. Sound words—like "crack," "pow" or "snap" can serve as a catalyst for creating original sound effects. Or use words that are associated with rhythm instruments and challenge children to come up with sounds using nontraditional sound sources that represent words like "jingle," "rattle," "ring" or "scrape."

Frequently there are places in stories where characters move or show emotion. Children can accompany the reader with vocal or instrumental sound effects. Look for words that can be repeated or echoed—this can emphasize important parts of the story. Some stories use language and phrases that can be accompanied by instruments, vocal or body percussion (snowflakes drifted down, softly, softly down). Use a quiet tinkling instrument such as a triangle or jingle bells or tone bells.

Some books have very obvious singable fragments. In *Time for Bed* by Mem Fox and Jane Dyer, the phrase "It's time for bed" is repeated throughout the story and would be an easy and lilting musical phrase that could be sung at the reader's discretion and comfort level. Students could be enlisted to create their own "song" phrases in books with many characters. Frequent opportunities for movement offer the possibility of full group participation and will keep children engaged and the story line energized. This can be as simple as gestures or fingerplays or can include more elaborate pantomime, staging or interpretive movement.

You also might consider adding an instrument or sound for various (or every) character in the story. After one reading of a story, challenge the children to help you choose or create a repetitive line for chanting for the next reading. Children can also create a sound environment for the story; using voices, bodies or instruments, invite the children to make up sounds that fit the setting.

## USING POETRY

Adding music, movement and dramatic inflection to poetry can make the poem come alive for students. These additions offer a dimension of personal engagement to the reader/performer. As children experience the poem in aural, visual and kinesthetic ways, the poem becomes a part of them. They are able to experience and express the emotion and changing moods of the poem. Additionally, because of the ensemble requirements of reading a poem "chorally," it is often a means to engage normally shy children.

Furthermore, participating as a "doer" of a poem is an excellent avenue to help children (and adults!) move beyond the oft-perceived barriers of poetry. Thus, the "doing" of a poem allows children to experience the rhythmic language, stretch their own rhythmic language and through their own participation broaden their understanding. Often, children will expand the writer's original vision and create their own new world of communication and meaning in a poem.

In your selection of a poem for choral reading, it is a good idea to select a work with repeated words or a recurring phrase. Look for places to insert solos—be sure to emphasize contrasting vocal inflections and rhythmic language. Add props such as scarves, streamers, puppets and instruments. Donna Moore, music resource teacher for the Albuquerque Public Schools, notes the following ways to enhance poetry.

Choral Readings

- Position speakers around the room
- Emphasize repeated words and phrases
- Use rhythmic language
- Explore inflections of the voice and different combinations of voices
- Explore opportunities for both choral and solo speaking

- Add introduction and coda
- Add repeated pattern ostinato
- Add background music or drumbeat
- Use vocal inflections or other vocal sounds as background
- Explore word play with key phrases and text

Movement and Drama

- Use tableaus
- Create/explore opportunities for pantomime
- Interpretive movement
- Locomotor and nonlocomotor movement

Musical Treatment

- Sound effects—vocal or instrumental
- Musical background or sound carpet
- Set the poem or parts of the poem to music (create a poem opera)
- Word play

## USING BACKGROUND MUSIC

Using a musical background creates a new dimension and added texture. It engages the children's listening at a deeper level and brings the stories to life in a magical way. This deeper engagement in the story inspires further exploration and extension of the story. For example, the children may want to act out the story or create their own movement to the recording. Or they may be inspired to play instruments to create their own musical setting. The story provides a meaningful and relevant context in which to engage with a variety of music, composers and performers.

In selecting recorded music to use with children's literature, use quality, time tested musical works (see Appendix C). It is important to consider the length and the mood of the story when choosing an accompanying piece of music. Be sure to include a variety of musical genres: jazz, classical, world beat, new age, bluegrass, rock, and so on. If you find it appropriate, share background information about the composer with the children.

It is almost always best to use instrumental music rather that music with words as a background or sound carpet. Music with lyrics can conflict with the story telling. It is important to practice reading the story with the music to master the timing. Using a digital counter or stopwatch will help synchronize the reading of the book with the musical background. Following are some suggestions compiled by Julia Church Hoffman.

| Book | Music |
|---|---|
| *Whistle for Willie* by Ezra Jack Keats | *Children's March* by Percy Grainger |
|  | *Creatures of the Garden* by Herbert Donaldson |
| *The Snowy Day* by Ezra Jack Keats | *Forgotten Dreams* by Leroy Anderson |
| *Snowmen at Night* by Caralyn Buehner & Mark Buehner | *Winter* (Allegro non olto & Largo) by Antonio Vivaldi (from *The Four Seasons*) |

*In the Garden with Van Gogh* by
    Julie Merbert and Suzanne Bober
*Don't Let the Pigeon Drive the Bus!*
    by Mo Willems

*Sliding* by Sandor Slomovits

*Carolina Shout* by James P. Johnson

## STORY DRAMATIZATION

Story dramatization, while not a purely "musical" endeavor, offers children another avenue by which to participate artistically with a piece of children's literature. This form of story drama promotes good listening skills, retention and comprehension and helps students predict event and storylines. Additionally, dramatization gives children a chance to develop sensory images of a particular character or seminal events of a story. As they portray characters and happenings, children begin to not only make conscious and unconscious connections with the book's characters and plot but also gain insight on the author's intentions and vision for the work (Blank Kelnor and Flynn, 2006).

When adding a dramatization to a story, it is important to set the stage with children by helping them understand they will have a chance to interact with and portray characters in a book. In order to do this effectively, children will have to analyze a character's personality traits, thoughts and feelings—and use their voices, bodies and actions to depict these qualities. Initially, as they create the dramatization, they will have to recall and retell the story in the correct sequence. Later, they might want to reorder the story—or change an ending.

Children who might be reluctant to sing or chant musically might feel comfortable using a different vocal quality or inflection in acting out a character. Story dramatization is also an excellent vehicle to encourage children to improvise or change the dialogue in a story. Character work like this is also an excellent springboard for trying out new postures, gestures or movements that reflect a certain character.

## MUSIC AND LANGUAGE ARTS CONNECTIONS

The following chart was created by Jan Delgado. It highlights music and language arts connections by presenting language arts performance standards (Albuquerque Public Schools, 2007) followed by musical connections and activities. Many of these musical connections/activities have been presented in this book.

| Literacy Skill | Musical Connection |
| --- | --- |
| *The Reading Process* | |
| Tracks left to right, top to bottom, uses story maps | Follows musical icons (listening maps). Identifies spaces between words: clapping beats, clapping rhythms |
| Develops phonemic awareness | Claps rhythm of the words, listens for and identifies specific sounds |
| Recognizes letters, alphabetic principal | Sings songs with same letter words, sing words in alphabetical order |
| Interprets information from diagrams, charts | Follows listening maps, follows musical notation |
| Reads and predicts repeated phrases or passages | Identifies and sings refrain of a song, sings and predicts cumulative songs |
| Adjusts reading speed | Moves, sings and plays instruments at different tempos |

Substitutes rhyming words

Sings songs with rhyming words, creating
rhyming endings to songs

*Reading Analysis*

Distinguishes among letters, words
and sentences

Reads or follows musical notation

Distinguishes among common forms,
identifies author's style

Identifies different styles of music

Plans and revises writing

Creates and refines an original composition

Uses predictability charts

Follows listening maps

Identifies setting, characters, important
events

Sings and analyzes a ballad, analyzes
patterns in music

Compares different versions of same story

Compares different styles of music

Dramatizes literature

Composes music, performs alone
and with others

Participates in peer editing

Performs original compositions, develops
constructive criticism skills

*Expressive Language Skills: Writing*

Spaces letters, has legible writing

Writes music using notation (using traditional
or created system) to fit beat spacing

Uses symbols to depict meaning

Draws pictures and musical symbols to depict
sounds

Sequences ideas

Identifies the beginning, middle and end of a
song

Identifies sentence structure

Identifies musical phrasing, singing and creating
call and response songs

Develops a topic sentence, writes a paragraph
with supporting details and elaboration

Identifies a musical theme structure, and
action, describing it in musical terms,
listening for theme and variation, composing

Uses narratives and descriptive writing

Uses music vocabulary to describe volume,
dynamics, tempo

*Expressive Language: Speaking*

Develops speech skills

Sings, explores vocal inflections, says
rhythmic speech pieces

Develops vocal inflection

Uses high and low pitched voices

Reads with good rhythm and pace

Keeps a steady beat

Develops skill with verbal and nonverbal
messages

Participates in action songs

Listens and views with focused attention

Listens for specific sounds that correspond
to specific actions or directions, using
listening maps

Listens to stories

Listens to songs (longer forms)

Follows instructions, responds to a variety
of media

Moves appropriately to different
musical sounds

*Research*

Sorts into categories, classifies

Categorizes various types of music, instruments,
movements

## IN CLOSING

It is clear that pairing musical activities with children's literature activates multiple learning modalities and gives students something to focus on visually, aurally and kinesthetically. When we add a "participation" or musical task to the presentation of a book, we are including more people in the storytelling, thus increasing the accessibility of the content. We know that repetition in structure, phrase and vocabulary help children become familiar with the repeating patterns and predictions. Musical activities, whether they come in the form of songs, games, dances or exploration of instruments can play an important role in helping children make connections with what they are learning.

Whenever we are able to incorporate music as a part of the daily life of a child, songs, rhythms and recordings become beloved treasures that teach. As children experience musical activities in conjunction with a piece of literature, key vocabulary, phrases and storylines become clues to unlocking a greater understanding of the world around them.

The lesson plans, strategies and rationales presented in this book are only a fraction of what is possible in thinking about the connection between music and children's books. These suggestions are simply to get teachers, librarians, childcare providers and home school educators *started* using music in their daily interactions with children. The sky is the limit in creative possibilities, and only you know what books, what musical activities and what kinds of lesson structures work best for you and your children.

The songs, recordings and musical activities we select will certainly reflect our own tastes and preferences, which is an effective avenue for connection with our students. We should also strive to explore the population of students that we are working with, including books, musical styles and materials that resonate with them. In keeping with my conviction and belief that all people can be musical in some way, I hope that the activities featured in this book are presented in an accessible, inclusive format.

Offering a child a chance to make music with a group can form a sense of belonging, of shared purpose. When we do music with children, we are in a sense helping them build their My Pod—their own repository of musical information. This then becomes an important basis for the way they make sense of the world.

## REFERENCES

Carle, Eric. *The Very Busy Spider.* New York: Philomel, 1995.

Dillon, Leo and Diane. *Rap a Tap Tap: Here's Bojangles—Think of That!* New York: Blue Sky Press, Scholastic, 2002.

Fox, Mem, and Jane Dyer. *Time for Bed.* San Diego, CA: Red Wagon Books, 1997.

Handy, Shirley. *MORE of the Singing Reading Connection: A Guide Exploring Key Elements and Activities Essential in Creating an Integrated, Brain Friendly Classroom.* Hilmar, CA: National Educational Network, 1998.

Igus, Toyomi, and Michele Wood. *I See the Rhythm.* San Francisco, CA: Children's Book Press, 1998.

Kelner, Lenore Blank, and Rosalind M. Flynn. *A Dramatic Approach to Reading Comprehension: Strategies and Activities for Classroom Teachers.* Portsmouth, NH: Heinemann, 2006.

McDermott, Gerald. *Papagayo the Mischief Maker.* New York: Harcourt, 1992.

Murray, Marjorie Dennis, and Patricia Wittmann. *Don't Wake Up the Bear.* New York: Marshall Cavendish Children's Books, 2006.

Sloan, Glenna. *Give Them Poetry: A Guide for Sharing Poetry with Children K–8.* New York: Teachers College Press, 2003.

# APPENDIX A

## *Glossary of Musical Terms*

The following terms are used in the lesson ideas and chapters in this book.

**A Cappella Singing:** singing unaccompanied by instruments.

**Action Words:** terms such as "crack, snap, pop, swipe" that suggest action.

**Ballad:** a song or a poem that tells a story, often in verse refrain form.

**Body Percussion:** involves the use of the body to make percussive sounds. This includes slapping, clapping, popping and stomping.

**Call and Response:** succession of two distinct phrases usually played or sung by different musicians, where the second phrase is heard as a direct commentary on or response to the first.

**Chest Voice:** Singing in the lower range; Sometimes referred to as belting.

**Choral Speaking:** the spoken recitation of poetry or prose by a chorus or group.

**Developmentally Appropriate Practice:** a perspective in early childhood education that emphasizes active learning experiences, varied instructional strategies, a balance between teacher and student centered activities, a fully integrated curriculum and the use of learning centers. A child's cultural background and his individual strengths are considered for entry points to learning.

**Expressive Musical Terms:** a list of musical terms that are likely to be encountered in printed scores which are generally meant to indicate pace, volume, mood and in some cases style.

**Falsetto:** an artificially high voice usually employed by men. The falsetto range requires more air and head resonance from the singer.

**Finger Cymbal:** small circular cymbals that usually have elastic straps for fingers.

**Fingerplay:** simple games usually played in early childhood settings where players show word meanings of songs and chants through simple actions and finger movements.

**Forte:** Expressive musical term (Italian term) that means loud.

**Found Instruments:** everyday objects such as keys, pencils, pots and pans that are used as nontraditional instruments for making percussive sounds.

**Glissando:** a musical term that refers to either a continuous sliding from one pitch to another (a "true" glissando), or an incidental scale played while moving from one melodic note to another (an "effective" glissando).

**Glockenspiel:** similar to the xylophone, in that it has tuned bars laid out in a fashion resembling a piano keyboard. A glockenspiel is much smaller and uses metal keys.

**Guiro:** a non-tuned percussion instrument that is held in the hand and played by scraping a stick along the ridged sides. The guiro is often heard in Latin music.

**Hand Drum:** any type of drum that is typically played by striking it with the bare hand rather than a stick, mallet, hammer or other type of beater. The simplest type of hand drum is the frame drum, which consists a shallow, cylindrical shell with a drumhead attached to one of the open ends.

**Head Voice:** a vocal technique used in singing to describe the resonance of singing something feeling to the singer as if it is occurring in their head.

**Jazz Chants:** chants and poems that use jazz rhythms to illustrate the natural stress and intonation patterns of conversational American English.

**Locomotor Movement:** refers to the movement from place to place and includes hopping, walking, running, jumping, leaping, skipping and galloping.

**Mezzo Forte:** an expressive musical term (from Italian) meaning medium loud.

**Mezzo Piano:** an expressive musical term (from Italian) meaning medium soft.

**Musical Form:** the structure or layout of a piece of music.

**Musical Notation:** a method used for writing down music.

**Nonlocomotor Movement:** refers to movement which is done in place such as bend, turn, twist, balance, stretch, push, pull, rock and sway.

**Ocean Drum:** a small hand drum with beads between two plastic heads.

**Ostinato:** a short repeated rhythmic pattern, tune or short melodic fragment.

**Piano:** an expressive musical term (from Italian) meaning soft.

**Pitch:** indicates the high or low position of a musical sound.

**Resonance:** the ringing quality of an instrument or voice that is produced through vibration.

**Rondo Form:** musical form where sections are repeated with contrasting sections interspersed.

**Rhythm Patterns:** an organization of rhythm groupings designed to make small nonmelodic motifs (in music) or versification (in poetry).

**Rhythm Soundpiece:** a rhythmic composition that has a distinct musical form.

**Shekere:** an African-derived rattle made of a large gourd with beads held by a string net on the outside.

**Singing Games:** often played by standing in a circle while singing the song, so they became known as ring games, which often pit multiple players against each other, or a single player against previous performances.

**Sound Carpet:** a subtle foundation of sound intended to provide musical support to a piece of music; the sound carpet often establishes a tonality and mood over which prominent themes or melodies are played.

**Sound Effects:** sounds (often used as background) that are created to enhance a story, poem, movie or film.

**Steady Beat:** a pulse in music that continues for an entire song or section of a piece of music.

**Story Recordings:** stories or works of literature that are recorded and read usually by actors. These recordings are sometimes enhanced or accompanied by music.

**Teasing Chant:** chanting or singing a limited range song that is based upon the minor third interval: sometimes known as the "sol-mi" chant.

**Treble Range:** range of notes that use the treble clef or G-clef. Most common range for children's voices.

**Vibration:** a throbbing effect in singing made by rapidly varying the breath pressure in singing.

**Xylophone:** a wooden barred instrument played with mallets.

# APPENDIX B

## Tunes Used in Lesson Ideas in Chapters 4–6

## Pizza Pizza Daddy-O

Call and Resonse Game Trad.

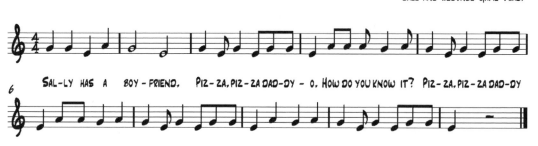

SAL-LY HAS A BOY-FRIEND, PIZ-ZA, PIZ-ZA DAD-DY - O. HOW DO YOU KNOW IT? PIZ-ZA, PIZ-ZA DAD-DY

O CAUSE SHE TOLD ME    PIZ-ZA, PIZ-ZA DAD-DY    OH LET'S ROCK IT    PIZ-ZA PIZ-ZA DAD-DY - O

## Follow the Drinkin' Gourd

WHEN THE    SUN COMES UP AND THE FIRST QUAIL CA-LLS    FOL-LOW____ THE

DRINK-IN' GOURD. THEN THE OLD MAN IS A WAIT-IN FOR TO CAR-RY YOU TO FREE-DOM    FOL-LOW THE DRIN-KIN

GOURD.    FOL-LOW____ THE DRIN-KIN' GOURD    -    FOL-LOW - THE____ DRINK-IN GOURD FOR THE____

OLD MAN IS A WAIT-IN' FOR TO CAR-RY YOU TO FREE-DOM    FOL-LOW THE DRINK'- IN GOURD

# APPENDIX C

# *Musical Works*

The following musical works can be purchased at most music stores or downloaded from the Internet.

## MUSICAL WORKS THAT PAIR WELL WITH CHILDREN'S LITERATURE

| Composer | Musical Work | Description |
| --- | --- | --- |
| Keiko Abe | Memories of Seashore | Marimba Solo |
| Leroy Anderson | Sleigh Ride | Orchestra |
| J. S. Bach | Brandenburg Concertos | Orchestra |
| J. S. Bach | Suite No. 3 in C Major for Unaccompanied Cello | Solo Cello |
| J. S. Bach | Toccata and Fugues in D Minor | Organ |
| Béla Bartók | Cradle Song | Violin Duet |
| Béla Bartók | Mikrokosmos | Contemporary Piano Pieces |
| Arthur Benjamin | Jamaican Rumba | Piano Duet |
| Ludwig van Beethoven | Sonata No. 14 in C-Sharp Minor, Moonlight Sonata | Piano Solo |
| Ludwig van Beethoven | Symphony No. 9 in D Minor, Ode to Joy, Movement 4 | Orchestra and Chorus |
| Leonard Bernstein | Overture to Candide | Orchestra |
| Johannes Brahms | Lullaby | Orchestra |
| Carlos Chavez | Toccata for Percussion | Percussion Instruments |
| Aaron Copland | Appalachian Spring | Orchestra |

| Composer | Musical Work | Description |
|----------|--------------|-------------|
| Aaron Copland | Billy the Kid | Orchestra |
| Aaron Copland | El Salon México | Orchestra |
| Claude Debussy | Children's Corner Suite | Orchestra |
| Claude Debussy | Claire de Lune | Piano Solo |
| Antonin Dvorák | Slavonic Dances | Orchestra |
| George Gershwin | Rhapsody in Blue | Orchestra |
| Morton Gould | Fanfare for Freedom | Orchestra |
| Percy Grainger | Lincolnshire Posey | Orchestra |
| Edvard Grieg | Peer Gynt Suite No. 1 | Orchestra |
| George Frideric Handel | Water Music | Orchestra |
| Gustav Holst | The Planets | Orchestra |
| Leos Janácek | Moravian Dance No. 2 | Orchestra |
| Wolfgang A. Mozart | Concerto in E-Flat | Horn and Orchestra |
| Wolfgang A. Mozart | Eine Kleine Nachtmusik | String Quartet |
| Modest Mussorgsky | Pictures at an Exhibition | Orchestra |
| Carl Orff | Carmina Burana | Orchestra and Chorus |
| Sergei Prokofiev | Lieutenant Kijé | Orchestra |
| Camille Saint-Saëns | Carnival of the Animals | Orchestra |
| Camille Saint-Saëns | Danse Macabre | Orchestra |
| John Philip Sousa | On Parade | Band |
| John Philip Sousa | Semper Fidelis | Band |
| John Philip Sousa | The Washington Post March | Band |
| John Philip Sousa | Stars and Stripes Forever | Band |
| Pitor Tchaikovsky | Nutcracker Suite | Orchestra |
| Pitor Tchaikovsky | 1812 Overture | Orchestra |
| Hector Villa-Lobos | Little Train of the Caipira | Orchestra |
| Antonio Vivaldi | Four Seasons | Orchestra |
| John Williams | Close Encounters of the Third Kind | Orchestra |
| Ralph Vaughan Williams | Fantasia on Greensleeves | Orchestra |

## JAZZ/SING/BLUES TITLES

A-Tisket A-Tasket
April Joy
Birdland
C-Jam Blues
Fascinatin' Rhythm
Flat Foot Floogee
God Bless the Child

Joe Turner Blues
Hit Me with a Hot Note and Watch Me Bounce
In the Mood
It Don't Mean a Thing if it Ain't Got That Swing
Mack the Knife
Maple Leaf Rag
Route 66
Saint Louis Blues
Summertime
Take Five
Take the "A" Train
The Entertainer
Watermelon Man
When the Saints Go Marching In

# APPENDIX D

# *Bibliography*

## BOOKS THAT SING!

Annotations by Donna Moore, Fine Arts Resource Teacher, Albuquerque Public Schools.

Cabrera, Jane. *Ten in the Bed*. New York: Holiday House, 2006.

Johnson, Paul Brett, lyrics by Tom Glazer. *On Top of Spaghetti*. New York: Scholastic, 2006.

Langstaff, John, and Nancy Winslow Parker. *Oh, A-Hunting We Will Go*. New York: Aladdin, 1991. "We'll catch a fox and put him in a box, and then we'll let him go!"

Mander, John. *Senor Don Gato*. Cambridge, MA: Candlewick Press, 2003.

Marsh, T. J., and Jennifer Ward, illustrated by Kenneth Spengler. *Somewhere in the Ocean*. Flagstaff, AZ: Rising Moon Books, 2000. Undersea version of "Over in the Meadow."

Marsh, T. J., and Jennifer Ward, illustrated by Kenneth Spengler. *Way Out in the Desert*. Flagstaff, AZ: Rising Moon Books, 1998. Southwest version of "Over in the Meadow."

Penner, Fred, and Renee Reichert. *The Cat Came Back*. New Milford, CT: Roaring Book Press, 2005.

Sturgess, Philemon, and Ashley Wolff. *She'll Be Comin' Round the Mountain*. New York: Little Brown, 2004. Southwest version.

Vaughan, Marcia, illustrated Pamela Lofts. *Wombat Stew*. Englewood Cliffs, NJ: Englewood Press, 1984. There is a recurring song in this book and the students can join you whenever Dingo says "Righto in they go!"

## "I KNOW AN OLD LADY" BOOKS

Colandro, Lucille, illustrated by Jared Lee. *There Was an Old Lady Who Swallowed a Bat!* New York: Scholastic, 2002.

Harper, Charise Mericle. *There Was a Bold Lady Who Wanted a Star*. Boston: Little, Brown, 2002. A variation on the traditional cumulative rhyme, a feisty woman tries roller skates, a bike and even a rocket to reach the stars.

Jackson, Alison, illustrated by Judith Byron Schachner. *I Know an Old Lady Who Swallowed a Pie*. New York: Puffin Books, 1997. The feast begins. After the pie, the old lady swallows a whole squash, all the salad and the entire turkey! Traditional Thanksgiving foods give a familiar new rhyme zing.

Karas, G. Brian. *I Know an Old Lady*. New York: Scholastic, 1994. By far the best part of this book is the illustrations. Older elementary children will love the book.

Sloat, Teri, illustrated by Reynold Ruffins. *There Was an Old Lady Who Swallowed a Trout!* New York: Henry Holt, 1998. This lady who swallowed a trout will lead the readers through a story capturing the scenery and wildlife of the Pacific Northwest.

## SOUNDS

Rammell, S. Kelly, and Jeanette Canyon. *City Beats: A Hip-hoppy Pigeon Poem.* Nevada City, CA: Dawn Publications, 2006. What is a day like for a pigeon? Sounds of the city.

Spier, Peter. *Crash, Bang, Boom. A Book of Sounds.* New York: Doubleday, 1990.

Wilson, Karma, and Suzanne Watts. *Hilda Must Be Dancing.* New York: Margaret K. McElderry Books, 2004. Hilda the Hippo loves to dance, but, Thumpety, Bump, Thumpety Bump, Boom! Bang! Bash! Can't she sing instead?

## MOVEMENT

Andrede, Giles, and Guy Parker-Rees. *Giraffes Can't Dance.* New York: Orchard Books, 1997. Gerald the giraffe can't dance, but he just needs to find his own music! Use your imagination about where to take this. A delight.

Ehlert, Lois. *Leaf Man.* New York: Harcourt, 2005. Use sounds to accompany the movement. Beautiful book of autumn leaves.

Jenkins, Steve, and Robin Page. *Move!* Boston: Houghton Mifflin, 2006. For very early grades. Ways animals move: leap, slither, dive, etc. Big pictures, big words.

## RHYTHMS

Lee, Spike, and Tonya Lewis Lee, illustrated by Kadir Nelson. *Please, Puppy, Please.* New York: Simon and Schuster, 2005. Variations of "Please, Puppy, Please" spoken in different rhythm patterns.

Webb, Steve. *Tanka, Tanka Skunk!* New York: Orchard Books, 2003. Great combination of animal names and rhythm.

## JAZZ/BLUES

Gollub, Matthew, and Karen Hanke. *Jazz Fly.* Santa Rosa, CA: Tortuga Press, 2000. What's the buzz? It's a fly who speaks jazz, and he's asking different critters which way to town.

London, Jonathan, and Woodleigh Hubbard. *Hip Cat.* San Francisco: Chronicle Press, 1993. A rhythmic text and brilliant illustrations bring alive where cool cats dig hot jazz.

Shahan, Sherry, and Mary Thelen. *The Jazzy Alphabet.* New York: Philomel Books, 2002. A hoppin', swingin', clip-clop-ringing, bebop-singing romp through the letters.

Shange, Ntozhake, and Romare Bearden. *I Live in Music.* New York: St. Martin's Press, 1994. Lyrical poem that is a tribute to the language of music and the magical, often mystical rhythms that connect people.

## BOOKS TO ENHANCE WITH MUSIC

Appelt, Kathy, and Jon Goodell. *Alley Cat's Meow.* New York: Harcourt, 2002. Starring "Red and Ginger." Red: He's dashing, smashing, a downtown kind of cat. He hopped on the A train and went downtown to a joint called The Alley Cat's Meow. Ginger: She's jazzy, snazzy, an uptown sort of gal. This book can be made into a rondo form, using rhythmic speech.

Krebs, Laurie, and Julia Cairns. *We All Went on Safari: A Counting Journey through Tanzania.* Boston, MA: Barefoot Books, 2001. This book can be sung. It can also be made into a cumulative form. Drumming can be used as an accompaniment. The back has explanations for the Swahili names, facts about Tanzania, information on the Masai and a counting chart in Swahili.

Kalan, Robert, and Byron Barton. *Jump, Frog Jump*! New York: William Morrow, 1981. Cumulative story with predictable repeated speech pattern. Each character may be represented by an instrument. Or all could play instruments on "jump, frog, jump." Students may also jump on those words.

Kimmel, Eric, and Janet Stevens. *Anansi and the Moss-Covered Rock.* New York: Holiday House, 1988. A favorite of my students. Use instrumental sound effects for the characters and on action words (e.g., "his head was spinning," use wind chimes, or use a xylophone bordun for walking). Do some acting out on the second reading, you can have the whole group, standing in random formation, acting out the actions of each character. The children particularly love to show Anansi falling down whenever he says the magic words.

Martin, Bill, Jr., John Archambault, and James Endicott. *Listen to the Rain*. New York: Henry Holt, 1988. The sounds of rain: the whisper, the slow soft sprinkle, the drip, drop tinkle. . . . The repeated pattern of this book can be sung. It can represent a rondo form.

Martin, Bill, Jr., and Eric Carle. *Polar Bear, Polar Bear, What Do You Hear?* New York: Henry Holt, 1991. Predictable book for the young ones. Represents pattern. This book can be sung.

Martin, Bill, Jr., and Eric Carle. *Panda Bear, Panda Bear, What Do You See?* New York: Henry Holt, 2003.

## POETRY

Mora, Pat, and Enrique O. Sanchez. *Confetti, Poems for Children*. New York: Lee & Low Books, 1996. Lovely Southwestern poems, mixing Spanish and English. "Colors Crackle, Colors Roar" connects color and sound. You can layer rhythms from the words for an ostinato.

Olaleye, Isaac, and Franc Lessac. *The Distant Talking Drum, Poems from Nigeria*. Honesdale, PA: Wordsong Books, 1995. Create rhythmic ostinati out of some of the words and phrases in the poem. Layer them. Transfer to African instruments and use as accompaniment for "Nigerian Boat" song or other African songs.

Prelutsky, Jack, and Garth Williams. *Ride a Purple Pelican*. New York: Greenwillow Books, 1986. A favorite. Short "place" poems for chanting, wordplay and layering word rhythms. My favorite is "Timble, Tamble Turkey."

# Index

Albuquerque Public Schools, 5, 93, 104, 106, 119

Bears: books on, 44; lesson ideas, 36–37, 39, 44, 76–77

Call and response, 61, 65, 70, 107, 109. *See also* Songs
Caregivers, 2–4, 9, 31–32, 36. *See also* Childcare providers
Chanting, 12–13, 19, 20–23, 28
Childcare providers, 1, 10, 57, 108. *See also* Caregivers
Choral reading, 5, 52, 83–84, 100–101, 104
Choral speaking, 22, 85, 96–97, 109

Delgado, Jan, 62, 77, 85, 96, 103
Delgado, Luis, 85, 94
Developmentally Appropriate Practice (DAP), 1, 4, 57, 109

Early literacy goals, 36; letter knowledge, 41; narrative skills, 42, 73; phonological awareness, 38, 42, 47–48, 50–51; predictions, 37; print awareness, 38, 41, 47–48, 51; print motivation, 73; rhyming words, 17, 21, 23, 52, 107; vocabulary, 42–43, 45, 57, 76, 85–86; word recognition, 5

Flanagan, Wilma, 44, 46, 53, 64, 68, 72

Haynes, Carla, 36, 42, 45, 47–48, 50, 62, 65, 79
Hoffman, Julia Church, 36, 38, 41, 51–52, 62, 66, 73, 80, 103, 105
Hutchinson, Sara, 85, 92–93

Infants, 2–3, 14, 26
Instruments: drums, 10, 19–20, 24–25, 34–35, 38–39, 42, 47–48, 50–51, 61–68, 74, 77, 85–90, 94, 103, 110, 120–21; found instruments, 21, 24, 85, 90, 103, 109; general, 8–9, 16, 22, 25, 34–39; glockenspiel, 16, 74, 110; pitched percussion, 73; rainstick, 25, 35, 62, 94; rhythm instruments, 19–21, 23–24, 35, 37, 60–63, 70, 77–79, 90–92, 95, 97, 103–4; xylophone, 16, 35, 81, 97–98, 110–11, 120
Improvisation, 32, 57, 75, 79, 92

Jazz, 85, 89, 90, 105, 116, 120; jazz chants, 23–24, 110

Language: acquisition, 1; development, 2, 4, 5
Learning centers, 1, 10, 109
Lullabies, 10, 22, 31, 33, 35–37, 43, 46, 67, 115. *See also* Toddlers

Mariachi, 85, 87–88
Martin, Kay, 62, 74, 76
Moore, Donna, 85, 90, 92, 103–4, 119
Movement: body percussion, 46, 62, 63, 76, 97; dancing, 8, 35, 61, 103; fingerplays, 33, 88, 109; locomotor/ nonlocomotor, 26–27, 29, 52, 61, 105, 110
Music Educators National Conference (MENC), 5
Musical concepts: dynamics, 22, 33, 63, 107; expressive terms, 63; form, 62, 79, 80, 110; general, 1, 3, 19, 21, 23, 26–29, 34–35; steady beat, 12, 21, 34, 38–39, 48–51, 53, 57–59, 61–62, 70, 75, 77–78, 86–87, 107, 110; tone color, 34, 36, 45

Nature: books on, 46; lesson ideas, 45

Ocean: books on, 68; lesson ideas, 66–67
Onomatopoeia, 22, 77, 89, 92

Pizza: books on, 72; lesson ideas, 70–71
Poetry, 1, 5, 20, 63, 65, 76, 92, 104, 109, 110, 121

Rain: books on, 63; lesson ideas, 62–63; poems, 63
Recorded music, 19, 21, 25–26, 35, 60, 67, 85, 88, 108, 111
Rhythmic speech, 19–21, 107, 120

Singing: exercises, 12–13; FAQ's, 13–17; how to, 11–12; general, 1–3, 5, 5–9; 9–10; intermediate grades, 83–85; primary grades, 58–59; toddlers, 32–33
Songs: ballad, 59, 82–84, 87–88, 100–101, 107, 109; call and response, 61, 65, 70, 107, 109; general, 1–12; how to teach, 14–17; story songs, 10, 58, 84
Sound carpet, 22, 25, 53, 68, 73, 103, 105, 110
Strickland, Christine, 85, 87, 89
Story time, 5, 19, 25–26, 36–37, 57

Toddlers, 14, 23, 31–36, 43
Toys: books on, 53–54; lesson ideas, 53

Vocal: exploration, 38; improvisation, 13; inflection, 21–22, 33, 45, 78, 103–7; modeling, 14, 84; percussion, 90, 103–4; range, 14–15; register, 12; sound effects, 104–5. *See also* Singing

Watkins, Regina Stella, 85, 95

Zero to Three, 5–6

# *About the Author*

REGINA CARLOW, Assistant Professor at the University of New Mexico, holds a bachelor's in music, a master of music degree from the Catholic University of America, and a Ph.D. from the University of Maryland, College Park. She teaches courses in elementary vocal and secondary choral methods and classes in early childhood education and teaching reading in the content area. She has been a K–12 music specialist and has taught in both university and community college settings.